Coffee Stains, Charcoal Smudges and Fried Eggs

Lithakazi Mkombe

Published by The JuxtaPlace, 2025.

COFFEE STAINS, CHARCOAL SMUDGES AND FRIED EGGS

First edition. March 20, 2025.

ISBN: 978-1037033056

Written by Lithakazi Mkombe.

To the woman reading this book:

You fight. You bleed. You win.

You're a lioness made to hunt.

You're a woman made to nurture.

Your instincts are ready to protect.

May your intimate battles nourish the bodies of your loved ones.

May you find words within this letter to heal you.

Preface

This is not the first book I write to you. All things I wrote to you were true, but allow me to be honest. You may wonder why I chose to write these words to you. Why I chose to lay bare to you the things that paint such an intimate story. I have always heard people ask others what their words would be if they were to write to their younger selves. I pondered this question one day and realized that I would write nothing, absolutely nothing. Having lived many years of life and managed to do the things I did I still appreciate the mystery - not knowing. (elaborate here)

Maybe not every part of it but every part that made me who I am. I have nothing to say to my younger self, nor do I have anything to say to the girl next year; but I have a lot to say about today. All I know is I have been fighting. I fight, I am very expressive and I do this using weapons closest to my heart. These are sometimes words, sometimes paint and sometimes movement.

Growing up I have always been the girl who spoke to herself or to cut holes in curtains seeking innovative ways for play. Evolving into adulthood needed me to lose this girl - which I refused to. A detriment. I believed there was no me without the things that spoke to my soul at the moment. Loudly they spoke of longevity, a guarantee to never lose relevance. They shaped my thoughts with feelings like I have been there; lived and loved. I heard them whispering songs that called me home in senses I never knew existed, covered in coffee stains, charcoal sumdges and fried eggs. I am led though. Feeling closer to the search of something deeper and something better. I understand that everyday lived could be a step closer or a step away from it, but these are my gems, they lead me, guiding me as I continue to find. A strange reality that every moment I breathe shapes are formed by the ink guiding and following our lives. Writing stories for the world to read. The writings

we did yesterday speaking of the state of th represent; nothing the past could imagine.

So I write this letter walking barefoot, immersed in art and not up to correcting my typos. Echoing in wonder of what would happen if we were not afraid or did not hide our weakness, our darkness.

There is so much more, I am a girl, black, previously disadvantaged and living in South Africa. I however walk places my feet cannot carry due to our progressive constitution. I do hope when faced with places my feet cannot carry like the gender and racial gap, my end is met by a miracle. That I understand that life, like sand on the ocean, cannot be contained or preplanned. It is unpredictable. Maybe you too have no letter for your younger self, or maybe you do. May these pages written in poetry to you help you write a story your fifty year old self will love to read - the best days of your life. Your life led by God. But I am here today.

There is a broken wooden bridge between the end of an era and the beginning of something greater - this part right here is that bridge for me. Behind you is a mountain that no one dared to climb. Glory is due even before you reach the top of it because of your work. You have done something no one was willing to. You tackled a mountain filled with heavy winds, rainfall, scorching heat and loneliness. Unpopular, isolated. Once you are at the top of it, feeling the rocks of the summit beneath your feet; you are covered in glory, glory due to you. There is a bridge you must cross - a determination of success. It is made of wood with broken pieces and torn-out strings from rope that is meant to hold it. The gender gap, the racial gap, all forms of inequality yet a progressive constitution pushes you. Bones filled with faith - for me in Jesus. You might die, you might live but across it is your reward - the reward of the climb. People never understand this moment. You have reached the mountaintop, all things should be well but they are not. They are instead worse. Never retreat. Cry, ask someone to hold your hand, close your eyes and do not forget to open them again. Continue

to walk and ignore the wind. On the other side is a plane - a pasture. It is the fruit of the breakthrough.

This is my story. I am crossing the bridge. It is that space between me receiving everything I have worked for - the funding, incubations, education, clients, etc, so I can afford my basic needs which at the moment seem like a big privilege. I have climbed the mountain. The wait between month-end to month-end when you do not know what you will eat or where you will stay but you are not retreating because you have climbed the mountain. On the other side is a pasture filled with security and rest for yourself, your children and your children's children. I am crossing the bridge with tears in my eyes; grabbing hands and closed eyes. I will remember to open them again. At the end of my closed out vision is the plane that was the price to begin with - not the glory of the mountain top but the freedom of my children. I should be free. I think I am free but I am lacking and I can attribute this to absolutely nothing. I have missed out because I am black, because I am a woman, because I am previously disadvantaged in a country with one of the most progressive constitutions in the world. Below I write my first poem for the book inspired by an art piece by Judith Mason - The Man who Sang and the Woman who Kept Silent (1998).

We are the memorials of your courage
Flying on local streets
In places silently designated
We hang, deserted, in barricading fences.
We are the memorials of your courage
Fighting on local streets
Swept from bins, parks and lonely forests...
Lithakazi Mkombe, 2025

Fried Eggs

Before we were woven into being in the wombs of our mothers, a beautiful story was written. Images crafted, sounds recorded, forming a beautiful musical piece. Uniquely worded, punctuated, on cahrcoal and paper and maybe oil on canvas, creative and academic - all different, bold and subtle; loud and quiet. We were then made, woven into sculptures, living, of Eden clay. Spun by Mighty hands, moistened by Living Waters and cured by His breath. Now Living figures and parts of His speech. What could not be expressed in words was spoken in pictures, what drawings couild not capture was painted in woprds. A vision only God could see, part of His divine mystery, nothing anyone could foresee. I am 30+, no husband, no prospect and strangely no friendships too.

I remember the day I walked into a second-hand bookshop and saw a Bible for R35. If you know me you know I cannot live without one but due to unforeseen reasons my daughter and I lost all our books and Bibles. Now, as a welcome to motherhood gift my big sister Dr. Kanyisa Mcina, gifted me with a new purple and pink NIV Mother's Bible. I have treasured and read it since. I knew where to find each scripture, on what page, paragraph and what highlighter I used on it. This could be because of my photographic memory. I kept it until it was holding on by the skin of its teeth. This is when I knew I needed a new one.

Being a girl means boys will ask for your hand in marriage often. If you know me, again, you know how I get so annoyed when a man asks to take me out on a date. As I grew older I started to wonder what if I miss my God-given husband because of this? Out of my need for a new Bible; trust in a powerful God and our ability to hear Him (He is always performing miracles for me and has gifted me with various gifts of the Spirit that I never talk about because I believe they are for function not fame.) I smiled at my Lord Jesus Christ and told Him that the man He has for me will definitely know within His heart of hearts

that he must get me a Bible. This is a "Can I take you out" gesture. Then I would know and say yes. My life is very imbalanced so I do not have time for dates and social activities. I do not mind this. I got ruined as an Architecture student. I am growing and I am looking to settle down. I have had my fair share of heartache inflicted on me by various people for various reasons. Some have scorned me, leaving my heart hardened. I bring my heart to God and ask Him to work on its ill-health so I can be a better person for myself, my child and future spouse one day but remember that I am grown and people are getting more evil. As I go on about my life I am reminded of something I once wrote.

As we go on about life we get to a place where we are looking at settling down. Where we may be faced with many prospects seeking our attention for marriage, to build a life together or to build a family together but the fear of choosing wrong can be crippling. We have preferences and expectations of how things should look like and what they will be. It is good to have expectations, please have standards. Do not fall into the trap of the world telling you that your standards are too high but be mindful of being unreal in setting them.

As I studied my Theology notes by the South African Theological Seminary I came across a unit in a module entitled Husbands. Although I thought there was nothing for me in that unit, I went through it for the sake of assessments but to my surprise it enlightened me to things that I may have taken for granted. It talks about the role of the husband at home towards his wife and children, and it led me to refining my choosing compass (checklist) by adding these four points of what a godly husband should look like at the top of my checklist.

There is a lot that can be said about a husband but I will focus on these three points and elaborate on one. He should lead, protect and provide for his wife. Below are a few notes on protection that I found we take for granted in our choosing.

Can he protect me:

Physically: Protect you from harm according to his means - set measures around the house, finances and other things that you find important to bring physical security.

Psychologically: Show you respect and acceptance. Treat you in kindness and love.

Philosophically: Initiate the Lord's way into counteracting the world with all its doctrines that seek to sweep humanity to and fro.

Spiritually: Lead you pastorally at home by initiating prayer and church attendance.

These four, more than physical appearances that change as the years progress, will remain within our hearts as things we are grateful for or as desires. Then I feel safe again. Protected and ready to continue my search.

Below I write about the injustices I have faced as a woman; injustices I have seen other woman face.

My story ios different. What strikes me is that it dioes not have to be pictures or wordfs; oil or charcoal, creative or academic - we are all different. We need to treat each other with kindness and compassion. Comnplimentary to each story being told. Different in gifting and ranking, yet equally important. May our lives paint the picture painted before time. We are living figures and parts of speech;embraced in the dictionary of life - the mouth of God that spoke this world into motion.

God is vast. His attributes can never be exhausted. Since the biginning of time angels and eldres stand in awe of Him. Since the beginning of time He has forever set ablaze a wonder unimagionable tio me that forces all my being to fall flat on the ground. Made in His image. A God who since eternity has struck angels with awe ibn revelation of who He is. Through us too, He wants to reveal His glory and one person will never be enough to embody even a single attribute of His. Our stories therefore are different. Let us not gravitate towards the norm. We are unique images of Him. We are searching, building

and trying to achieve our dreams. Sometimes we run ahead of Him to stroke in lines. He is full of grace and by it He erases our errors with His love restroking His original image - a restoration of our destinies. So maybe mine is to be a spinster, or to marry and be without kids but a godly desire within me calls me unto these. Yet these are stories I cannot write on my own. In episodes of depressiobn, hurt and sometimes hope I write the poetry below to the rhythm of my frying eggs.

Charcoal Smudges

When I think about the giftings and talents God has given me and the stewardship of them I think of the story of divine humility. This involves deity who formed an earthen vessel with limitations and filled it with His life so it lives past its sell by date with the ability to steward many talents (the 10 talent servant). Earthenware susceptible to dents and cracks, yet always welcome at the table of the Potter. This Potter who, when He fixes us spuins us in control, control that can be daunting to eyes that see nearer than they should. This is who God says we are. This is who I believe I am. Handmade by God the Potter, smelling of rainy spring mornings and approved - marked by a glorious seal.

As I continue with my life I rested in knowing that the fight isn't in the size of my boots but the size of the Spirit of the Potter within me. It is He who fights. He gives me the ability to stand in mockery because He, Himself was given a crown of thorns in shame because His garments were stripped. In a lowly status because saw dust was the gist of His career.

Coffee Stains

When the sound of the flute at the constitution Hill (the place I regard as home for me because that is where all the hope of our citizens lies, the home that protects our rights and encourages us to responsibility in protecting the rights of others.) at the Human Rights Festival in March 2024 during my technical rehearsal hit the stage I held back tears. It was at that moment that I knew why I worked myself to the bone.

I continue to grow. I do not know who I will be next year but I do have bigger dreams than I had last year. I am always reminded that birds of a feather flock together. I am mindful of people I surround myself with - the things I read. You are the scents of the people that surround you. In my quest to pursue my greatest potential I have also learnt to be silent, to listen more, to let people hear my smile, feel the warmth in my absence and to show up in the mystery. UI am lovingly selective of the company I keep.

I have a new trend now - I read a lot of biographies of people who I believe have a similar background to mine but have achieved greatness beyond measure.

God has shown me kindness. I believe in teh scripture that if you submit your plans to Him, He will make your paths straight. In 2024 I could not believe that I was featured as one of 50 most influential women in South Africa. This, following my making Business and Arts South Africa's Top 20, Arts and Culture Trust Top 30, North West University Top 3 and GIBS Buisness School's Festival of Ideas Top 12. I have not even scratched the surface with what I want to achieve with my life.

I have managed to birth ON Read App - a reading and publishing app; 1 Old Note; The JuxtaPlace; Printed Honey - these are all companies that have been recognized by different companies including the most respected Durban Chamber of Commerce.

My work is mainly on justice - economic freedom for women, literacy and bridging the language gap, freedom for Africans.

I was especially honoured and i bleiev it is only the beginning when I got the opportunity to conduct research for teh United Nations Department of Economic Development when I got my interview invitation. I was drenched in the Theatre du Soleil Nomadic School for Collaborative Practices in creating Theatre and shortlisted for the North West University Pitch-Your-Business competition Pitch. Shortly after, I had an interview with the Cultural Attache (Diplomat), Secretary General and Deputy Secretary General of the French Institute of South Africa in Braamfontein for their final interview for the Cultural Projects Officer post. I saw how God's leading was amazibng.

By Imnene Mkombe
This one goes to my favourite
The one above the rest
The most awesome, kindest person
This lady she's the best
Even though this year was different
Full of troubles I might add
I'm just happy we went through it
With God's help, for this I'm glad
And even though this year was different
Not as fun as I had hoped
Thanks to you I won't detest it
I won't sit around and mope
We've lost family, we've lost friends
A lot of ties came to an end
We've still got Jesus
You've got me
So we're as happy as can be
Well Merry Christmas to you mum!
And have a happy new year
Good luck with 2025
From the one you hold dear.

Preface

This is not the first book I write to you. All things I wrote to you were true, but allow me to be honest. You may wonder why I chose to write these words to you. Why I chose to lay bare to you the things that paint such an intimate story. I have always heard people ask others what their words would be if they were to write to their younger selves. I pondered this question one day and realized that I would write nothing, absolutely nothing. Having lived many years of life and managed to do the things I did I still appreciate the mystery - not knowing. (elaborate here)

Maybe not every part of it but every part that made me who I am. I have nothing to say to my younger self, nor do I have anything to say to the girl next year; but I have a lot to say about today. All I know is I have been fighting. I fight, I am very expressive and I do this using weapons closest to my heart. These are sometimes words, sometimes paint and sometimes movement.

Growing up I have always been the girl who spoke to herself or to cut holes in curtains seeking innovative ways for play. Evolving into adulthood needed me to lose this girl - which I refused to. A detriment. I believed there was no me without the things that spoke to my soul at the moment. Loudly they spoke of longevity, a guarantee to never lose relevance. They shaped my thoughts with feelings like I have been there; lived and loved. I heard them whispering songs that called me home in senses I never knew existed, covered in coffee stains, charcoal sumdges and fried eggs. I am led though. Feeling closer to the search of something deeper and something better. I understand that everyday lived could be a step closer or a step away from it, but these are my gems, they lead me, guiding me as I continue to find. A strange reality that every moment I breathe shapes are formed by the ink guiding and following our lives. Writing stories for the world to read. The writings

we did yesterday speaking of the state of th represent; nothing the past could imagine.

So I write this letter walking barefoot, immersed in art and not up to correcting my typos. Echoing in wonder of what would happen if we were not afraid or did not hide our weakness, our darkness.

There is so much more, I am a girl, black, previously disadvantaged and living in South Africa. I however walk places my feet cannot carry due to our progressive constitution. I do hope when faced with places my feet cannot carry like the gender and racial gap, my end is met by a miracle. That I understand that life, like sand on the ocean, cannot be contained or preplanned. It is unpredictable. Maybe you too have no letter for your younger self, or maybe you do. May these pages written in poetry to you help you write a story your fifty year old self will love to read - the best days of your life. Your life led by God. But I am here today.

There is a broken wooden bridge between the end of an era and the beginning of something greater - this part right here is that bridge for me. Behind you is a mountain that no one dared to climb. Glory is due even before you reach the top of it because of your work. You have done something no one was willing to. You tackled a mountain filled with heavy winds, rainfall, scorching heat and loneliness. Unpopular, isolated. Once you are at the top of it, feeling the rocks of the summit beneath your feet; you are covered in glory, glory due to you. There is a bridge you must cross - a determination of success. It is made of wood with broken pieces and torn-out strings from rope that is meant to hold it. The gender gap, the racial gap, all forms of inequality yet a progressive constitution pushes you. Bones filled with faith - for me in Jesus. You might die, you might live but across it is your reward - the reward of the climb. People never understand this moment. You have reached the mountaintop, all things should be well but they are not. They are instead worse. Never retreat. Cry, ask someone to hold your hand, close your eyes and do not forget to open them again. Continue

to walk and ignore the wind. On the other side is a plane - a pasture. It is the fruit of the breakthrough.

This is my story. I am crossing the bridge. It is that space between me receiving everything I have worked for - the funding, incubations, education, clients, etc, so I can afford my basic needs which at the moment seem like a big privilege. I have climbed the mountain. The wait between month-end to month-end when you do not know what you will eat or where you will stay but you are not retreating because you have climbed the mountain. On the other side is a pasture filled with security and rest for yourself, your children and your children's children. I am crossing the bridge with tears in my eyes; grabbing hands and closed eyes. I will remember to open them again. At the end of my closed out vision is the plane that was the price to begin with - not the glory of the mountain top but the freedom of my children. I should be free. I think I am free but I am lacking and I can attribute this to absolutely nothing. I have missed out because I am black, because I am a woman, because I am previously disadvantaged in a country with one of the most progressive constitutions in the world. Below I write my first poem for the book inspired by an art piece by Judith Mason - The Man who Sang and the Woman who Kept Silent (1998).

We are the memorials of your courage
Flying on local streets
In places silently designated
We hang, deserted, in barricading fences.
We are the memorials of your courage
Fighting on local streets
Swept from bins, parks and lonely forests...
Lithakazi Mkombe, 2025

Fried Eggs

Before we were woven into being in the wombs of our mothers, a beautiful story was written. Images crafted, sounds recorded, forming a beautiful musical piece. Uniquely worded, punctuated, on cahrcoal and paper and maybe oil on canvas, creative and academic - all different, bold and subtle; loud and quiet. We were then made, woven into sculptures, living, of Eden clay. Spun by Mighty hands, moistened by Living Waters and cured by His breath. Now Living figures and parts of His speech. What could not be expressed in words was spoken in pictures, what drawings couild not capture was painted in woprds. A vision only God could see, part of His divine mystery, nothing anyone could foresee. I am 30+, no husband, no prospect and strangely no friendships too.

I remember the day I walked into a second-hand bookshop and saw a Bible for R35. If you know me you know I cannot live without one but due to unforeseen reasons my daughter and I lost all our books and Bibles. Now, as a welcome to motherhood gift my big sister Dr. Kanyisa Mcina, gifted me with a new purple and pink NIV Mother's Bible. I have treasured and read it since. I knew where to find each scripture, on what page, paragraph and what highlighter I used on it. This could be because of my photographic memory. I kept it until it was holding on by the skin of its teeth. This is when I knew I needed a new one.

Being a girl means boys will ask for your hand in marriage often. If you know me, again, you know how I get so annoyed when a man asks to take me out on a date. As I grew older I started to wonder what if I miss my God-given husband because of this? Out of my need for a new Bible; trust in a powerful God and our ability to hear Him (He is always performing miracles for me and has gifted me with various gifts of the Spirit that I never talk about because I believe they are for function not fame.) I smiled at my Lord Jesus Christ and told Him that the man He has for me will definitely know within His heart of hearts

that he must get me a Bible. This is a "Can I take you out" gesture. Then I would know and say yes. My life is very imbalanced so I do not have time for dates and social activities. I do not mind this. I got ruined as an Architecture student. I am growing and I am looking to settle down. I have had my fair share of heartache inflicted on me by various people for various reasons. Some have scorned me, leaving my heart hardened. I bring my heart to God and ask Him to work on its ill-health so I can be a better person for myself, my child and future spouse one day but remember that I am grown and people are getting more evil. As I go on about my life I am reminded of something I once wrote.

As we go on about life we get to a place where we are looking at settling down. Where we may be faced with many prospects seeking our attention for marriage, to build a life together or to build a family together but the fear of choosing wrong can be crippling. We have preferences and expectations of how things should look like and what they will be. It is good to have expectations, please have standards. Do not fall into the trap of the world telling you that your standards are too high but be mindful of being unreal in setting them.

As I studied my Theology notes by the South African Theological Seminary I came across a unit in a module entitled Husbands. Although I thought there was nothing for me in that unit, I went through it for the sake of assessments but to my surprise it enlightened me to things that I may have taken for granted. It talks about the role of the husband at home towards his wife and children, and it led me to refining my choosing compass (checklist) by adding these four points of what a godly husband should look like at the top of my checklist.

There is a lot that can be said about a husband but I will focus on these three points and elaborate on one. He should lead, protect and provide for his wife. Below are a few notes on protection that I found we take for granted in our choosing.

Can he protect me:

Physically: Protect you from harm according to his means - set measures around the house, finances and other things that you find important to bring physical security.

Psychologically: Show you respect and acceptance. Treat you in kindness and love.

Philosophically: Initiate the Lord's way into counteracting the world with all its doctrines that seek to sweep humanity to and fro.

Spiritually: Lead you pastorally at home by initiating prayer and church attendance.

These four, more than physical appearances that change as the years progress, will remain within our hearts as things we are grateful for or as desires. Then I feel safe again. Protected and ready to continue my search.

Below I write about the injustices I have faced as a woman; injustices I have seen other woman face.

My story ios different. What strikes me is that it dioes not have to be pictures or wordfs; oil or charcoal, creative or academic - we are all different. We need to treat each other with kindness and compassion. Comnplimentary to each story being told. Different in gifting and ranking, yet equally important. May our lives paint the picture painted before time. We are living figures and parts of speech;embraced in the dictionary of life - the mouth of God that spoke this world into motion.

God is vast. His attributes can never be exhausted. Since the biginning of time angels and eldres stand in awe of Him. Since the beginning of time He has forever set ablaze a wonder unimagionable tio me that forces all my being to fall flat on the ground. Made in His image. A God who since eternity has struck angels with awe ibn revelation of who He is. Through us too, He wants to reveal His glory and one person will never be enough to embody even a single attribute of His. Our stories therefore are different. Let us not gravitate towards the norm. We are unique images of Him. We are searching, building

and trying to achieve our dreams. Sometimes we run ahead of Him to stroke in lines. He is full of grace and by it He erases our errors with His love restroking His original image - a restoration of our destinies. So maybe mine is to be a spinster, or to marry and be without kids but a godly desire within me calls me unto these. Yet these are stories I cannot write on my own. In episodes of depressiobn, hurt and sometimes hope I write the poetry below to the rhythm of my frying eggs.

Charcoal Smudges

When I think about the giftings and talents God has given me and the stewardship of them I think of the story of divine humility. This involves deity who formed an earthen vessel with limitations and filled it with His life so it lives past its sell by date with the ability to steward many talents (the 10 talent servant). Earthenware susceptible to dents and cracks, yet always welcome at the table of the Potter. This Potter who, when He fixes us spuins us in control, control that can be daunting to eyes that see nearer than they should. This is who God says we are. This is who I believe I am. Handmade by God the Potter, smelling of rainy spring mornings and approved - marked by a glorious seal.

As I continue with my life I rested in knowing that the fight isn't in the size of my boots but the size of the Spirit of the Potter within me. It is He who fights. He gives me the ability to stand in mockery because He, Himself was given a crown of thorns in shame because His garments were stripped. In a lowly status because saw dust was the gist of His career.

Coffee Stains

When the sound of the flute at the constitution Hill (the place I regard as home for me because that is where all the hope of our citizens lies, the home that protects our rights and encourages us to responsibility in protecting the rights of others.) at the Human Rights Festival in March 2024 during my technical rehearsal hit the stage I held back tears. It was at that moment that I knew why I worked myself to the bone.

I continue to grow. I do not know who I will be next year but I do have bigger dreams than I had last year. I am always reminded that birds of a feather flock together. I am mindful of people I surround myself with - the things I read. You are the scents of the people that surround you. In my quest to pursue my greatest potential I have also learnt to be silent, to listen more, to let people hear my smile, feel the warmth in my absence and to show up in the mystery. UI am lovingly selective of the company I keep.

I have a new trend now - I read a lot of biographies of people who I believe have a similar background to mine but have achieved greatness beyond measure.

God has shown me kindness. I believe in teh scripture that if you submit your plans to Him, He will make your paths straight. In 2024 I could not believe that I was featured as one of 50 most influential women in South Africa. This, following my making Business and Arts South Africa's Top 20, Arts and Culture Trust Top 30, North West University Top 3 and GIBS Buisness School's Festival of Ideas Top 12. I have not even scratched the surface with what I want to achieve with my life.

I have managed to birth ON Read App - a reading and publishing app; 1 Old Note; The JuxtaPlace; Printed Honey - these are all companies that have been recognized by different companies including the most respected Durban Chamber of Commerce.

My work is mainly on justice - economic freedom for women, literacy and bridging the language gap, freedom for Africans.

I was especially honoured and i bleiev it is only the beginning when I got the opportunity to conduct research for teh United Nations Department of Economic Development when I got my interview invitation. I was drenched in the Theatre du Soleil Nomadic School for Collaborative Practices in creating Theatre and shortlisted for the North West University Pitch-Your-Business competition Pitch. Shortly after, I had an interview with the Cultural Attache (Diplomat), Secretary General and Deputy Secretary General of the French Institute of South Africa in Braamfontein for their final interview for the Cultural Projects Officer post. I saw how God's leading was amazibng.

By Imnene Mkombe
This one goes to my favourite
The one above the rest
The most awesome, kindest person
This lady she's the best
Even though this year was different
Full of troubles I might add
I'm just happy we went through it
With God's help, for this I'm glad
And even though this year was different
Not as fun as I had hoped
Thanks to you I won't detest it
I won't sit around and mope
We've lost family, we've lost friends
A lot of ties came to an end
We've still got Jesus
You've got me
So we're as happy

Preface

This is not the first book I write to you. All things I wrote to you were true, but allow me to be honest. You may wonder why I chose to write these words to you. Why I chose to lay bare to you the things that paint such an intimate story. I have always heard people ask others what their words would be if they were to write to their younger selves. I pondered this question one day and realized that I would write nothing, absolutely nothing. Having lived many years of life and managed to do the things I did I still appreciate the mystery - not knowing. (elaborate here)

Maybe not every part of it but every part that made me who I am. I have nothing to say to my younger self, nor do I have anything to say to the girl next year; but I have a lot to say about today. All I know is I have been fighting. I fight, I am very expressive and I do this using weapons closest to my heart. These are sometimes words, sometimes paint and sometimes movement.

Growing up I have always been the girl who spoke to herself or to cut holes in curtains seeking innovative ways for play. Evolving into adulthood needed me to lose this girl - which I refused to. A detriment. I believed there was no me without the things that spoke to my soul at the moment. Loudly they spoke of longevity, a guarantee to never lose relevance. They shaped my thoughts with feelings like I have been there; lived and loved. I heard them whispering songs that called me home in senses I never knew existed, covered in coffee stains, charcoal sumdges and fried eggs. I am led though. Feeling closer to the search of something deeper and something better. I understand that everyday lived could be a step closer or a step away from it, but these are my gems, they lead me, guiding me as I continue to find. A strange reality that every moment I breathe shapes are formed by the ink guiding and following our lives. Writing stories for the world to read. The writings

we did yesterday speaking of the state of th represent; nothing the past could imagine.

So I write this letter walking barefoot, immersed in art and not up to correcting my typos. Echoing in wonder of what would happen if we were not afraid or did not hide our weakness, our darkness.

There is so much more, I am a girl, black, previously disadvantaged and living in South Africa. I however walk places my feet cannot carry due to our progressive constitution. I do hope when faced with places my feet cannot carry like the gender and racial gap, my end is met by a miracle. That I understand that life, like sand on the ocean, cannot be contained or preplanned. It is unpredictable. Maybe you too have no letter for your younger self, or maybe you do. May these pages written in poetry to you help you write a story your fifty year old self will love to read - the best days of your life. Your life led by God. But I am here today.

There is a broken wooden bridge between the end of an era and the beginning of something greater - this part right here is that bridge for me. Behind you is a mountain that no one dared to climb. Glory is due even before you reach the top of it because of your work. You have done something no one was willing to. You tackled a mountain filled with heavy winds, rainfall, scorching heat and loneliness. Unpopular, isolated. Once you are at the top of it, feeling the rocks of the summit beneath your feet; you are covered in glory, glory due to you. There is a bridge you must cross - a determination of success. It is made of wood with broken pieces and torn-out strings from rope that is meant to hold it. The gender gap, the racial gap, all forms of inequality yet a progressive constitution pushes you. Bones filled with faith - for me in Jesus. You might die, you might live but across it is your reward - the reward of the climb. People never understand this moment. You have reached the mountaintop, all things should be well but they are not. They are instead worse. Never retreat. Cry, ask someone to hold your hand, close your eyes and do not forget to open them again. Continue

to walk and ignore the wind. On the other side is a plane - a pasture. It is the fruit of the breakthrough.

This is my story. I am crossing the bridge. It is that space between me receiving everything I have worked for - the funding, incubations, education, clients, etc, so I can afford my basic needs which at the moment seem like a big privilege. I have climbed the mountain. The wait between month-end to month-end when you do not know what you will eat or where you will stay but you are not retreating because you have climbed the mountain. On the other side is a pasture filled with security and rest for yourself, your children and your children's children. I am crossing the bridge with tears in my eyes; grabbing hands and closed eyes. I will remember to open them again. At the end of my closed out vision is the plane that was the price to begin with - not the glory of the mountain top but the freedom of my children. I should be free. I think I am free but I am lacking and I can attribute this to absolutely nothing. I have missed out because I am black, because I am a woman, because I am previously disadvantaged in a country with one of the most progressive constitutions in the world. Below I write my first poem for the book inspired by an art piece by Judith Mason - The Man who Sang and the Woman who Kept Silent (1998).

We are the memorials of your courage
Flying on local streets
In places silently designated
We hang, deserted, in barricading fences.
We are the memorials of your courage
Fighting on local streets
Swept from bins, parks and lonely forests...
Lithakazi Mkombe, 2025

Fried Eggs

Before we were woven into being in the wombs of our mothers, a beautiful story was written. Images crafted, sounds recorded, forming a beautiful musical piece. Uniquely worded, punctuated, on cahrcoal and paper and maybe oil on canvas, creative and academic - all different, bold and subtle; loud and quiet. We were then made, woven into sculptures, living, of Eden clay. Spun by Mighty hands, moistened by Living Waters and cured by His breath. Now Living figures and parts of His speech. What could not be expressed in words was spoken in pictures, what drawings couild not capture was painted in woprds. A vision only God could see, part of His divine mystery, nothing anyone could foresee. I am 30+, no husband, no prospect and strangely no friendships too.

I remember the day I walked into a second-hand bookshop and saw a Bible for R35. If you know me you know I cannot live without one but due to unforeseen reasons my daughter and I lost all our books and Bibles. Now, as a welcome to motherhood gift my big sister Dr. Kanyisa Mcina, gifted me with a new purple and pink NIV Mother's Bible. I have treasured and read it since. I knew where to find each scripture, on what page, paragraph and what highlighter I used on it. This could be because of my photographic memory. I kept it until it was holding on by the skin of its teeth. This is when I knew I needed a new one.

Being a girl means boys will ask for your hand in marriage often. If you know me, again, you know how I get so annoyed when a man asks to take me out on a date. As I grew older I started to wonder what if I miss my God-given husband because of this? Out of my need for a new Bible; trust in a powerful God and our ability to hear Him (He is always performing miracles for me and has gifted me with various gifts of the Spirit that I never talk about because I believe they are for function not fame.) I smiled at my Lord Jesus Christ and told Him that the man He has for me will definitely know within His heart of hearts

that he must get me a Bible. This is a "Can I take you out" gesture. Then I would know and say yes. My life is very imbalanced so I do not have time for dates and social activities. I do not mind this. I got ruined as an Architecture student. I am growing and I am looking to settle down. I have had my fair share of heartache inflicted on me by various people for various reasons. Some have scorned me, leaving my heart hardened. I bring my heart to God and ask Him to work on its ill-health so I can be a better person for myself, my child and future spouse one day but remember that I am grown and people are getting more evil. As I go on about my life I am reminded of something I once wrote.

As we go on about life we get to a place where we are looking at settling down. Where we may be faced with many prospects seeking our attention for marriage, to build a life together or to build a family together but the fear of choosing wrong can be crippling. We have preferences and expectations of how things should look like and what they will be. It is good to have expectations, please have standards. Do not fall into the trap of the world telling you that your standards are too high but be mindful of being unreal in setting them.

As I studied my Theology notes by the South African Theological Seminary I came across a unit in a module entitled Husbands. Although I thought there was nothing for me in that unit, I went through it for the sake of assessments but to my surprise it enlightened me to things that I may have taken for granted. It talks about the role of the husband at home towards his wife and children, and it led me to refining my choosing compass (checklist) by adding these four points of what a godly husband should look like at the top of my checklist.

There is a lot that can be said about a husband but I will focus on these three points and elaborate on one. He should lead, protect and provide for his wife. Below are a few notes on protection that I found we take for granted in our choosing.

Can he protect me:

Physically: Protect you from harm according to his means - set measures around the house, finances and other things that you find important to bring physical security.

Psychologically: Show you respect and acceptance. Treat you in kindness and love.

Philosophically: Initiate the Lord's way into counteracting the world with all its doctrines that seek to sweep humanity to and fro.

Spiritually: Lead you pastorally at home by initiating prayer and church attendance.

These four, more than physical appearances that change as the years progress, will remain within our hearts as things we are grateful for or as desires. Then I feel safe again. Protected and ready to continue my search.

Below I write about the injustices I have faced as a woman; injustices I have seen other woman face.

My story ios different. What strikes me is that it dioes not have to be pictures or wordfs; oil or charcoal, creative or academic - we are all different. We need to treat each other with kindness and compassion. Comnplimentary to each story being told. Different in gifting and ranking, yet equally important. May our lives paint the picture painted before time. We are living figures and parts of speech;embraced in the dictionary of life - the mouth of God that spoke this world into motion.

God is vast. His attributes can never be exhausted. Since the biginning of time angels and eldres stand in awe of Him. Since the beginning of time He has forever set ablaze a wonder unimagionable tio me that forces all my being to fall flat on the ground. Made in His image. A God who since eternity has struck angels with awe ibn revelation of who He is. Through us too, He wants to reveal His glory and one person will never be enough to embody even a single attribute of His. Our stories therefore are different. Let us not gravitate towards the norm. We are unique images of Him. We are searching, building

and trying to achieve our dreams. Sometimes we run ahead of Him to stroke in lines. He is full of grace and by it He erases our errors with His love restroking His original image - a restoration of our destinies. So maybe mine is to be a spinster, or to marry and be without kids but a godly desire within me calls me unto these. Yet these are stories I cannot write on my own. In episodes of depressiobn, hurt and sometimes hope I write the poetry below to the rhythm of my frying eggs.

Charcoal Smudges

When I think about the giftings and talents God has given me and the stewardship of them I think of the story of divine humility. This involves deity who formed an earthen vessel with limitations and filled it with His life so it lives past its sell by date with the ability to steward many talents (the 10 talent servant). Earthenware susceptible to dents and cracks, yet always welcome at the table of the Potter. This Potter who, when He fixes us spuins us in control, control that can be daunting to eyes that see nearer than they should. This is who God says we are. This is who I believe I am. Handmade by God the Potter, smelling of rainy spring mornings and approved - marked by a glorious seal.

As I continue with my life I rested in knowing that the fight isn't in the size of my boots but the size of the Spirit of the Potter within me. It is He who fights. He gives me the ability to stand in mockery because He, Himself was given a crown of thorns in shame because His garments were stripped. In a lowly status because saw dust was the gist of His career.

Coffee Stains

When the sound of the flute at the constitution Hill (the place I regard as home for me because that is where all the hope of our citizens lies, the home that protects our rights and encourages us to responsibility in protecting the rights of others.) at the Human Rights Festival in March 2024 during my technical rehearsal hit the stage I held back tears. It was at that moment that I knew why I worked myself to the bone.

I continue to grow. I do not know who I will be next year but I do have bigger dreams than I had last year. I am always reminded that birds of a feather flock together. I am mindful of people I surround myself with - the things I read. You are the scents of the people that surround you. In my quest to pursue my greatest potential I have also learnt to be silent, to listen more, to let people hear my smile, feel the warmth in my absence and to show up in the mystery. UI am lovingly selective of the company I keep.

I have a new trend now - I read a lot of biographies of people who I believe have a similar background to mine but have achieved greatness beyond measure.

God has shown me kindness. I believe in teh scripture that if you submit your plans to Him, He will make your paths straight. In 2024 I could not believe that I was featured as one of 50 most influential women in South Africa. This, following my making Business and Arts South Africa's Top 20, Arts and Culture Trust Top 30, North West University Top 3 and GIBS Buisness School's Festival of Ideas Top 12. I have not even scratched the surface with what I want to achieve with my life.

I have managed to birth ON Read App - a reading and publishing app; 1 Old Note; The JuxtaPlace; Printed Honey - these are all companies that have been recognized by different companies including the most respected Durban Chamber of Commerce.

My work is mainly on justice - economic freedom for women, literacy and bridging the language gap, freedom for Africans.

I was especially honoured and i bleiev it is only the beginning when I got the opportunity to conduct research for teh United Nations Department of Economic Development when I got my interview invitation. I was drenched in the Theatre du Soleil Nomadic School for Collaborative Practices in creating Theatre and shortlisted for the North West University Pitch-Your-Business competition Pitch. Shortly after, I had an interview with the Cultural Attache (Diplomat), Secretary General and Deputy Secretary General of the French Institute of South Africa in Braamfontein for their final interview for the Cultural Projects Officer post. I saw how God's leading was amazibng.

By Imnene Mkombe
This one goes to my favourite
The one above the rest
The most awesome, kindest person
This lady she's the best
Even though this year was different
Full of troubles I might add
I'm just happy we went through it
With God's help, for this I'm glad
And even though this year was different
Not as fun as I had hoped
Thanks to you I won't detest it
I won't sit around and mope
We've lost family, we've lost friends
A lot of ties came to an end
We've still got Jesus
You've got me
So we're as happy

Preface

This is not the first book I write to you. All things I wrote to you were true, but allow me to be honest. You may wonder why I chose to write these words to you. Why I chose to lay bare to you the things that paint such an intimate story. I have always heard people ask others what their words would be if they were to write to their younger selves. I pondered this question one day and realized that I would write nothing, absolutely nothing. Having lived many years of life and managed to do the things I did I still appreciate the mystery - not knowing. (elaborate here)

Maybe not every part of it but every part that made me who I am. I have nothing to say to my younger self, nor do I have anything to say to the girl next year; but I have a lot to say about today. All I know is I have been fighting. I fight, I am very expressive and I do this using weapons closest to my heart. These are sometimes words, sometimes paint and sometimes movement.

Growing up I have always been the girl who spoke to herself or to cut holes in curtains seeking innovative ways for play. Evolving into adulthood needed me to lose this girl - which I refused to. A detriment. I believed there was no me without the things that spoke to my soul at the moment. Loudly they spoke of longevity, a guarantee to never lose relevance. They shaped my thoughts with feelings like I have been there; lived and loved. I heard them whispering songs that called me home in senses I never knew existed, covered in coffee stains, charcoal sumdges and fried eggs. I am led though. Feeling closer to the search of something deeper and something better. I understand that everyday lived could be a step closer or a step away from it, but these are my gems, they lead me, guiding me as I continue to find. A strange reality that every moment I breathe shapes are formed by the ink guiding and following our lives. Writing stories for the world to read. The writings

we did yesterday speaking of the state of th represent; nothing the past could imagine.

So I write this letter walking barefoot, immersed in art and not up to correcting my typos. Echoing in wonder of what would happen if we were not afraid or did not hide our weakness, our darkness.

There is so much more, I am a girl, black, previously disadvantaged and living in South Africa. I however walk places my feet cannot carry due to our progressive constitution. I do hope when faced with places my feet cannot carry like the gender and racial gap, my end is met by a miracle. That I understand that life, like sand on the ocean, cannot be contained or preplanned. It is unpredictable. Maybe you too have no letter for your younger self, or maybe you do. May these pages written in poetry to you help you write a story your fifty year old self will love to read - the best days of your life. Your life led by God. But I am here today.

There is a broken wooden bridge between the end of an era and the beginning of something greater - this part right here is that bridge for me. Behind you is a mountain that no one dared to climb. Glory is due even before you reach the top of it because of your work. You have done something no one was willing to. You tackled a mountain filled with heavy winds, rainfall, scorching heat and loneliness. Unpopular, isolated. Once you are at the top of it, feeling the rocks of the summit beneath your feet; you are covered in glory, glory due to you. There is a bridge you must cross - a determination of success. It is made of wood with broken pieces and torn-out strings from rope that is meant to hold it. The gender gap, the racial gap, all forms of inequality yet a progressive constitution pushes you. Bones filled with faith - for me in Jesus. You might die, you might live but across it is your reward - the reward of the climb. People never understand this moment. You have reached the mountaintop, all things should be well but they are not. They are instead worse. Never retreat. Cry, ask someone to hold your hand, close your eyes and do not forget to open them again. Continue

to walk and ignore the wind. On the other side is a plane - a pasture. It is the fruit of the breakthrough.

This is my story. I am crossing the bridge. It is that space between me receiving everything I have worked for - the funding, incubations, education, clients, etc, so I can afford my basic needs which at the moment seem like a big privilege. I have climbed the mountain. The wait between month-end to month-end when you do not know what you will eat or where you will stay but you are not retreating because you have climbed the mountain. On the other side is a pasture filled with security and rest for yourself, your children and your children's children. I am crossing the bridge with tears in my eyes; grabbing hands and closed eyes. I will remember to open them again. At the end of my closed out vision is the plane that was the price to begin with - not the glory of the mountain top but the freedom of my children. I should be free. I think I am free but I am lacking and I can attribute this to absolutely nothing. I have missed out because I am black, because I am a woman, because I am previously disadvantaged in a country with one of the most progressive constitutions in the world. Below I write my first poem for the book inspired by an art piece by Judith Mason - The Man who Sang and the Woman who Kept Silent (1998).

We are the memorials of your courage
Flying on local streets
In places silently designated
We hang, deserted, in barricading fences.
We are the memorials of your courage
Fighting on local streets
Swept from bins, parks and lonely forests...
Lithakazi Mkombe, 2025

Fried Eggs

Before we were woven into being in the wombs of our mothers, a beautiful story was written. Images crafted, sounds recorded, forming a beautiful musical piece. Uniquely worded, punctuated, on cahrcoal and paper and maybe oil on canvas, creative and academic - all different, bold and subtle; loud and quiet. We were then made, woven into sculptures, living, of Eden clay. Spun by Mighty hands, moistened by Living Waters and cured by His breath. Now Living figures and parts of His speech. What could not be expressed in words was spoken in pictures, what drawings couild not capture was painted in woprds. A vision only God could see, part of His divine mystery, nothing anyone could foresee. I am 30+, no husband, no prospect and strangely no friendships too.

I remember the day I walked into a second-hand bookshop and saw a Bible for R35. If you know me you know I cannot live without one but due to unforeseen reasons my daughter and I lost all our books and Bibles. Now, as a welcome to motherhood gift my big sister Dr. Kanyisa Mcina, gifted me with a new purple and pink NIV Mother's Bible. I have treasured and read it since. I knew where to find each scripture, on what page, paragraph and what highlighter I used on it. This could be because of my photographic memory. I kept it until it was holding on by the skin of its teeth. This is when I knew I needed a new one.

Being a girl means boys will ask for your hand in marriage often. If you know me, again, you know how I get so annoyed when a man asks to take me out on a date. As I grew older I started to wonder what if I miss my God-given husband because of this? Out of my need for a new Bible; trust in a powerful God and our ability to hear Him (He is always performing miracles for me and has gifted me with various gifts of the Spirit that I never talk about because I believe they are for function not fame.) I smiled at my Lord Jesus Christ and told Him that the man He has for me will definitely know within His heart of hearts

that he must get me a Bible. This is a "Can I take you out" gesture. Then I would know and say yes. My life is very imbalanced so I do not have time for dates and social activities. I do not mind this. I got ruined as an Architecture student. I am growing and I am looking to settle down. I have had my fair share of heartache inflicted on me by various people for various reasons. Some have scorned me, leaving my heart hardened. I bring my heart to God and ask Him to work on its ill-health so I can be a better person for myself, my child and future spouse one day but remember that I am grown and people are getting more evil. As I go on about my life I am reminded of something I once wrote.

As we go on about life we get to a place where we are looking at settling down. Where we may be faced with many prospects seeking our attention for marriage, to build a life together or to build a family together but the fear of choosing wrong can be crippling. We have preferences and expectations of how things should look like and what they will be. It is good to have expectations, please have standards. Do not fall into the trap of the world telling you that your standards are too high but be mindful of being unreal in setting them.

As I studied my Theology notes by the South African Theological Seminary I came across a unit in a module entitled Husbands. Although I thought there was nothing for me in that unit, I went through it for the sake of assessments but to my surprise it enlightened me to things that I may have taken for granted. It talks about the role of the husband at home towards his wife and children, and it led me to refining my choosing compass (checklist) by adding these four points of what a godly husband should look like at the top of my checklist.

There is a lot that can be said about a husband but I will focus on these three points and elaborate on one. He should lead, protect and provide for his wife. Below are a few notes on protection that I found we take for granted in our choosing.

Can he protect me:

Physically: Protect you from harm according to his means - set measures around the house, finances and other things that you find important to bring physical security.

Psychologically: Show you respect and acceptance. Treat you in kindness and love.

Philosophically: Initiate the Lord's way into counteracting the world with all its doctrines that seek to sweep humanity to and fro.

Spiritually: Lead you pastorally at home by initiating prayer and church attendance.

These four, more than physical appearances that change as the years progress, will remain within our hearts as things we are grateful for or as desires. Then I feel safe again. Protected and ready to continue my search.

Below I write about the injustices I have faced as a woman; injustices I have seen other woman face.

My story ios different. What strikes me is that it dioes not have to be pictures or wordfs; oil or charcoal, creative or academic - we are all different. We need to treat each other with kindness and compassion. Comnplimentary to each story being told. Different in gifting and ranking, yet equally important. May our lives paint the picture painted before time. We are living figures and parts of speech;embraced in the dictionary of life - the mouth of God that spoke this world into motion.

God is vast. His attributes can never be exhausted. Since the biginning of time angels and eldres stand in awe of Him. Since the beginning of time He has forever set ablaze a wonder unimagionable tio me that forces all my being to fall flat on the ground. Made in His image. A God who since eternity has struck angels with awe ibn revelation of who He is. Through us too, He wants to reveal His glory and one person will never be enough to embody even a single attribute of His. Our stories therefore are different. Let us not gravitate towards the norm. We are unique images of Him. We are searching, building

and trying to achieve our dreams. Sometimes we run ahead of Him to stroke in lines. He is full of grace and by it He erases our errors with His love restroking His original image - a restoration of our destinies. So maybe mine is to be a spinster, or to marry and be without kids but a godly desire within me calls me unto these. Yet these are stories I cannot write on my own. In episodes of depressiobn, hurt and sometimes hope I write the poetry below to the rhythm of my frying eggs.

Charcoal Smudges

When I think about the giftings and talents God has given me and the stewardship of them I think of the story of divine humility. This involves deity who formed an earthen vessel with limitations and filled it with His life so it lives past its sell by date with the ability to steward many talents (the 10 talent servant). Earthenware susceptible to dents and cracks, yet always welcome at the table of the Potter. This Potter who, when He fixes us spuins us in control, control that can be daunting to eyes that see nearer than they should. This is who God says we are. This is who I believe I am. Handmade by God the Potter, smelling of rainy spring mornings and approved - marked by a glorious seal.

As I continue with my life I rested in knowing that the fight isn't in the size of my boots but the size of the Spirit of the Potter within me. It is He who fights. He gives me the ability to stand in mockery because He, Himself was given a crown of thorns in shame because His garments were stripped. In a lowly status because saw dust was the gist of His career.

Coffee Stains

When the sound of the flute at the constitution Hill (the place I regard as home for me because that is where all the hope of our citizens lies, the home that protects our rights and encourages us to responsibility in protecting the rights of others.) at the Human Rights Festival in March 2024 during my technical rehearsal hit the stage I held back tears. It was at that moment that I knew why I worked myself to the bone.

I continue to grow. I do not know who I will be next year but I do have bigger dreams than I had last year. I am always reminded that birds of a feather flock together. I am mindful of people I surround myself with - the things I read. You are the scents of the people that surround you. In my quest to pursue my greatest potential I have also learnt to be silent, to listen more, to let people hear my smile, feel the warmth in my absence and to show up in the mystery. UI am lovingly selective of the company I keep.

I have a new trend now - I read a lot of biographies of people who I believe have a similar background to mine but have achieved greatness beyond measure.

God has shown me kindness. I believe in teh scripture that if you submit your plans to Him, He will make your paths straight. In 2024 I could not believe that I was featured as one of 50 most influential women in South Africa. This, following my making Business and Arts South Africa's Top 20, Arts and Culture Trust Top 30, North West University Top 3 and GIBS Buisness School's Festival of Ideas Top 12. I have not even scratched the surface with what I want to achieve with my life.

I have managed to birth ON Read App - a reading and publishing app; 1 Old Note; The JuxtaPlace; Printed Honey - these are all companies that have been recognized by different companies including the most respected Durban Chamber of Commerce.

My work is mainly on justice - economic freedom for women, literacy and bridging the language gap, freedom for Africans.

I was especially honoured and i bleiev it is only the beginning when I got the opportunity to conduct research for teh United Nations Department of Economic Development when I got my interview invitation. I was drenched in the Theatre du Soleil Nomadic School for Collaborative Practices in creating Theatre and shortlisted for the North West University Pitch-Your-Business competition Pitch. Shortly after, I had an interview with the Cultural Attache (Diplomat), Secretary General and Deputy Secretary General of the French Institute of South Africa in Braamfontein for their final interview for the Cultural Projects Officer post. I saw how God's leading was amazibng.

By Imnene Mkombe
This one goes to my favourite
The one above the rest
The most awesome, kindest person
This lady she's the best
Even though this year was different
Full of troubles I might add
I'm just happy we went through it
With God's help, for this I'm glad
And even though this year was different
Not as fun as I had hoped
Thanks to you I won't detest it
I won't sit around and mope
We've lost family, we've lost friends
A lot of ties came to an end
We've still got Jesus
You've got me
So we're as happy

Preface

This is not the first book I write to you. All things I wrote to you were true, but allow me to be honest. You may wonder why I chose to write these words to you. Why I chose to lay bare to you the things that paint such an intimate story. I have always heard people ask others what their words would be if they were to write to their younger selves. I pondered this question one day and realized that I would write nothing, absolutely nothing. Having lived many years of life and managed to do the things I did I still appreciate the mystery - not knowing. (elaborate here)

Maybe not every part of it but every part that made me who I am. I have nothing to say to my younger self, nor do I have anything to say to the girl next year; but I have a lot to say about today. All I know is I have been fighting. I fight, I am very expressive and I do this using weapons closest to my heart. These are sometimes words, sometimes paint and sometimes movement.

Growing up I have always been the girl who spoke to herself or to cut holes in curtains seeking innovative ways for play. Evolving into adulthood needed me to lose this girl - which I refused to. A detriment, I believed there was no me without the things that spoke to my soul at the moment. Loudly they spoke of longevity, a guarantee to never lose relevance. They shaped my thoughts with feelings like I have been there; lived and loved. I heard them whispering songs that called me home in senses I never knew existed, covered in coffee stains, charcoal sumdges and fried eggs. I am led though. Feeling closer to the search of something deeper and something better. I understand that everyday lived could be a step closer or a step away from it, but these are my gems, they lead me, guiding me as I continue to find. A strange reality that every moment I breathe shapes are formed by the ink guiding and following our lives. Writing stories for the world to read. The writings

we did yesterday speaking of the state of th represent; nothing the past could imagine.

So I write this letter walking barefoot, immersed in art and not up to correcting my typos. Echoing in wonder of what would happen if we were not afraid or did not hide our weakness, our darkness.

There is so much more, I am a girl, black, previously disadvantaged and living in South Africa. I however walk places my feet cannot carry due to our progressive constitution. I do hope when faced with places my feet cannot carry like the gender and racial gap, my end is met by a miracle. That I understand that life, like sand on the ocean, cannot be contained or preplanned. It is unpredictable. Maybe you too have no letter for your younger self, or maybe you do. May these pages written in poetry to you help you write a story your fifty year old self will love to read - the best days of your life. Your life led by God. But I am here today.

There is a broken wooden bridge between the end of an era and the beginning of something greater - this part right here is that bridge for me. Behind you is a mountain that no one dared to climb. Glory is due even before you reach the top of it because of your work. You have done something no one was willing to. You tackled a mountain filled with heavy winds, rainfall, scorching heat and loneliness. Unpopular, isolated. Once you are at the top of it, feeling the rocks of the summit beneath your feet; you are covered in glory, glory due to you. There is a bridge you must cross - a determination of success. It is made of wood with broken pieces and torn-out strings from rope that is meant to hold it. The gender gap, the racial gap, all forms of inequality yet a progressive constitution pushes you. Bones filled with faith - for me in Jesus. You might die, you might live but across it is your reward - the reward of the climb. People never understand this moment. You have reached the mountaintop, all things should be well but they are not. They are instead worse. Never retreat. Cry, ask someone to hold your hand, close your eyes and do not forget to open them again. Continue

to walk and ignore the wind. On the other side is a plane - a pasture. It is the fruit of the breakthrough.

This is my story. I am crossing the bridge. It is that space between me receiving everything I have worked for - the funding, incubations, education, clients, etc, so I can afford my basic needs which at the moment seem like a big privilege. I have climbed the mountain. The wait between month-end to month-end when you do not know what you will eat or where you will stay but you are not retreating because you have climbed the mountain. On the other side is a pasture filled with security and rest for yourself, your children and your children's children. I am crossing the bridge with tears in my eyes; grabbing hands and closed eyes. I will remember to open them again. At the end of my closed out vision is the plane that was the price to begin with - not the glory of the mountain top but the freedom of my children. I should be free. I think I am free but I am lacking and I can attribute this to absolutely nothing. I have missed out because I am black, because I am a woman, because I am previously disadvantaged in a country with one of the most progressive constitutions in the world. Below I write my first poem for the book inspired by an art piece by Judith Mason - The Man who Sang and the Woman who Kept Silent (1998).

We are the memorials of your courage
Flying on local streets
In places silently designated
We hang, deserted, in barricading fences.
We are the memorials of your courage
Fighting on local streets
Swept from bins, parks and lonely forests...
Lithakazi Mkombe, 2025

Fried Eggs

Before we were woven into being in the wombs of our mothers, a beautiful story was written. Images crafted, sounds recorded, forming a beautiful musical piece. Uniquely worded, punctuated, on cahrcoal and paper and maybe oil on canvas, creative and academic - all different, bold and subtle; loud and quiet. We were then made, woven into sculptures, living, of Eden clay. Spun by Mighty hands, moistened by Living Waters and cured by His breath. Now Living figures and parts of His speech. What could not be expressed in words was spoken in pictures, what drawings couild not capture was painted in woprds. A vision only God could see, part of His divine mystery, nothing anyone could foresee. I am 30+, no husband, no prospect and strangely no friendships too.

I remember the day I walked into a second-hand bookshop and saw a Bible for R35. If you know me you know I cannot live without one but due to unforeseen reasons my daughter and I lost all our books and Bibles. Now, as a welcome to motherhood gift my big sister Dr. Kanyisa Mcina, gifted me with a new purple and pink NIV Mother's Bible. I have treasured and read it since. I knew where to find each scripture, on what page, paragraph and what highlighter I used on it. This could be because of my photographic memory. I kept it until it was holding on by the skin of its teeth. This is when I knew I needed a new one.

Being a girl means boys will ask for your hand in marriage often. If you know me, again, you know how I get so annoyed when a man asks to take me out on a date. As I grew older I started to wonder what if I miss my God-given husband because of this? Out of my need for a new Bible; trust in a powerful God and our ability to hear Him (He is always performing miracles for me and has gifted me with various gifts of the Spirit that I never talk about because I believe they are for function not fame.) I smiled at my Lord Jesus Christ and told Him that the man He has for me will definitely know within His heart of hearts

that he must get me a Bible. This is a "Can I take you out" gesture. Then I would know and say yes. My life is very imbalanced so I do not have time for dates and social activities. I do not mind this. I got ruined as an Architecture student. I am growing and I am looking to settle down. I have had my fair share of heartache inflicted on me by various people for various reasons. Some have scorned me, leaving my heart hardened. I bring my heart to God and ask Him to work on its ill-health so I can be a better person for myself, my child and future spouse one day but remember that I am grown and people are getting more evil. As I go on about my life I am reminded of something I once wrote.

As we go on about life we get to a place where we are looking at settling down. Where we may be faced with many prospects seeking our attention for marriage, to build a life together or to build a family together but the fear of choosing wrong can be crippling. We have preferences and expectations of how things should look like and what they will be. It is good to have expectations, please have standards. Do not fall into the trap of the world telling you that your standards are too high but be mindful of being unreal in setting them.

As I studied my Theology notes by the South African Theological Seminary I came across a unit in a module entitled Husbands. Although I thought there was nothing for me in that unit, I went through it for the sake of assessments but to my surprise it enlightened me to things that I may have taken for granted. It talks about the role of the husband at home towards his wife and children, and it led me to refining my choosing compass (checklist) by adding these four points of what a godly husband should look like at the top of my checklist.

There is a lot that can be said about a husband but I will focus on these three points and elaborate on one. He should lead, protect and provide for his wife. Below are a few notes on protection that I found we take for granted in our choosing.

Can he protect me:

Physically: Protect you from harm according to his means - set measures around the house, finances and other things that you find important to bring physical security.

Psychologically: Show you respect and acceptance. Treat you in kindness and love.

Philosophically: Initiate the Lord's way into counteracting the world with all its doctrines that seek to sweep humanity to and fro.

Spiritually: Lead you pastorally at home by initiating prayer and church attendance.

These four, more than physical appearances that change as the years progress, will remain within our hearts as things we are grateful for or as desires. Then I feel safe again. Protected and ready to continue my search.

Below I write about the injustices I have faced as a woman; injustices I have seen other woman face.

My story ios different. What strikes me is that it dioes not have to be pictures or wordfs; oil or charcoal, creative or academic - we are all different. We need to treat each other with kindness and compassion. Comnplimentary to each story being told. Different in gifting and ranking, yet equally important. May our lives paint the picture painted before time. We are living figures and parts of speech;embraced in the dictionary of life - the mouth of God that spoke this world into motion.

God is vast. His attributes can never be exhausted. Since the biginning of time angels and eldres stand in awe of Him. Since the beginning of time He has forever set ablaze a wonder unimagionable tio me that forces all my being to fall flat on the ground. Made in His image. A God who since eternity has struck angels with awe ibn revelation of who He is. Through us too, He wants to reveal His glory and one person will never be enough to embody even a single attribute of His. Our stories therefore are different. Let us not gravitate towards the norm. We are unique images of Him. We are searching, building

and trying to achieve our dreams. Sometimes we run ahead of Him to stroke in lines. He is full of grace and by it He erases our errors with His love restroking His original image - a restoration of our destinies. So maybe mine is to be a spinster, or to marry and be without kids but a godly desire within me calls me unto these. Yet these are stories I cannot write on my own. In episodes of depressiobn, hurt and sometimes hope I write the poetry below to the rhythm of my frying eggs.

Charcoal Smudges

When I think about the giftings and talents God has given me and the stewardship of them I think of the story of divine humility. This involves deity who formed an earthen vessel with limitations and filled it with His life so it lives past its sell by date with the ability to steward many talents (the 10 talent servant). Earthenware susceptible to dents and cracks, yet always welcome at the table of the Potter. This Potter who, when He fixes us spuins us in control, control that can be daunting to eyes that see nearer than they should. This is who God says we are. This is who I believe I am. Handmade by God the Potter, smelling of rainy spring mornings and approved - marked by a glorious seal.

As I continue with my life I rested in knowing that the fight isn't in the size of my boots but the size of the Spirit of the Potter within me. It is He who fights. He gives me the ability to stand in mockery because He, Himself was given a crown of thorns in shame because His garments were stripped. In a lowly status because saw dust was the gist of His career.

Coffee Stains

When the sound of the flute at the constitution Hill (the place I regard as home for me because that is where all the hope of our citizens lies, the home that protects our rights and encourages us to responsibility in protecting the rights of others.) at the Human Rights Festival in March 2024 during my technical rehearsal hit the stage I held back tears. It was at that moment that I knew why I worked myself to the bone.

I continue to grow. I do not know who I will be next year but I do have bigger dreams than I had last year. I am always reminded that birds of a feather flock together. I am mindful of people I surround myself with - the things I read. You are the scents of the people that surround you. In my quest to pursue my greatest potential I have also learnt to be silent, to listen more, to let people hear my smile, feel the warmth in my absence and to show up in the mystery. UI am lovingly selective of the company I keep.

I have a new trend now - I read a lot of biographies of people who I believe have a similar background to mine but have achieved greatness beyond measure.

God has shown me kindness. I believe in teh scripture that if you submit your plans to Him, He will make your paths straight. In 2024 I could not believe that I was featured as one of 50 most influential women in South Africa. This, following my making Business and Arts South Africa's Top 20, Arts and Culture Trust Top 30, North West University Top 3 and GIBS Buisness School's Festival of Ideas Top 12. I have not even scratched the surface with what I want to achieve with my life.

I have managed to birth ON Read App - a reading and publishing app; 1 Old Note; The JuxtaPlace; Printed Honey - these are all companies that have been recognized by different companies including the most respected Durban Chamber of Commerce.

My work is mainly on justice - economic freedom for women, literacy and bridging the language gap, freedom for Africans.

I was especially honoured and i bleiev it is only the beginning when I got the opportunity to conduct research for teh United Nations Department of Economic Development when I got my interview invitation. I was drenched in the Theatre du Soleil Nomadic School for Collaborative Practices in creating Theatre and shortlisted for the North West University Pitch-Your-Business competition Pitch. Shortly after, I had an interview with the Cultural Attache (Diplomat), Secretary General and Deputy Secretary General of the French Institute of South Africa in Braamfontein for their final interview for the Cultural Projects Officer post. I saw how God's leading was amazibng.

By Imnene Mkombe
This one goes to my favourite
The one above the rest
The most awesome, kindest person
This lady she's the best
Even though this year was different
Full of troubles I might add
I'm just happy we went through it
With God's help, for this I'm glad
And even though this year was different
Not as fun as I had hoped
Thanks to you I won't detest it
I won't sit around and mope
We've lost family, we've lost friends
A lot of ties came to an end
We've still got Jesus
You've got me
So we're as happy

Preface

This is not the first book I write to you. All things I wrote to you were true, but allow me to be honest. You may wonder why I chose to write these words to you. Why I chose to lay bare to you the things that paint such an intimate story. I have always heard people ask others what their words would be if they were to write to their younger selves. I pondered this question one day and realized that I would write nothing, absolutely nothing. Having lived many years of life and managed to do the things I did I still appreciate the mystery - not knowing. (elaborate here)

Maybe not every part of it but every part that made me who I am. I have nothing to say to my younger self, nor do I have anything to say to the girl next year; but I have a lot to say about today. All I know is I have been fighting. I fight, I am very expressive and I do this using weapons closest to my heart. These are sometimes words, sometimes paint and sometimes movement.

Growing up I have always been the girl who spoke to herself or to cut holes in curtains seeking innovative ways for play. Evolving into adulthood needed me to lose this girl - which I refused to. A detriment. I believed there was no me without the things that spoke to my soul at the moment. Loudly they spoke of longevity, a guarantee to never lose relevance. They shaped my thoughts with feelings like I have been there; lived and loved. I heard them whispering songs that called me home in senses I never knew existed, covered in coffee stains, charcoal sumdges and fried eggs. I am led though. Feeling closer to the search of something deeper and something better. I understand that everyday lived could be a step closer or a step away from it, but these are my gems, they lead me, guiding me as I continue to find. A strange reality that every moment I breathe shapes are formed by the ink guiding and following our lives. Writing stories for the world to read. The writings

we did yesterday speaking of the state of th represent; nothing the past could imagine.

So I write this letter walking barefoot, immersed in art and not up to correcting my typos. Echoing in wonder of what would happen if we were not afraid or did not hide our weakness, our darkness.

There is so much more, I am a girl, black, previously disadvantaged and living in South Africa. I however walk places my feet cannot carry due to our progressive constitution. I do hope when faced with places my feet cannot carry like the gender and racial gap, my end is met by a miracle. That I understand that life, like sand on the ocean, cannot be contained or preplanned. It is unpredictable. Maybe you too have no letter for your younger self, or maybe you do. May these pages written in poetry to you help you write a story your fifty year old self will love to read - the best days of your life. Your life led by God. But I am here today.

There is a broken wooden bridge between the end of an era and the beginning of something greater - this part right here is that bridge for me. Behind you is a mountain that no one dared to climb. Glory is due even before you reach the top of it because of your work. You have done something no one was willing to. You tackled a mountain filled with heavy winds, rainfall, scorching heat and loneliness. Unpopular, isolated. Once you are at the top of it, feeling the rocks of the summit beneath your feet; you are covered in glory, glory due to you. There is a bridge you must cross - a determination of success. It is made of wood with broken pieces and torn-out strings from rope that is meant to hold it. The gender gap, the racial gap, all forms of inequality yet a progressive constitution pushes you. Bones filled with faith - for me in Jesus. You might die, you might live but across it is your reward - the reward of the climb. People never understand this moment. You have reached the mountaintop, all things should be well but they are not. They are instead worse. Never retreat. Cry, ask someone to hold your hand, close your eyes and do not forget to open them again. Continue

to walk and ignore the wind. On the other side is a plane - a pasture. It is the fruit of the breakthrough.

This is my story. I am crossing the bridge. It is that space between me receiving everything I have worked for - the funding, incubations, education, clients, etc, so I can afford my basic needs which at the moment seem like a big privilege. I have climbed the mountain. The wait between month-end to month-end when you do not know what you will eat or where you will stay but you are not retreating because you have climbed the mountain. On the other side is a pasture filled with security and rest for yourself, your children and your children's children. I am crossing the bridge with tears in my eyes; grabbing hands and closed eyes. I will remember to open them again. At the end of my closed out vision is the plane that was the price to begin with - not the glory of the mountain top but the freedom of my children. I should be free. I think I am free but I am lacking and I can attribute this to absolutely nothing. I have missed out because I am black, because I am a woman, because I am previously disadvantaged in a country with one of the most progressive constitutions in the world. Below I write my first poem for the book inspired by an art piece by Judith Mason - The Man who Sang and the Woman who Kept Silent (1998).

We are the memorials of your courage
Flying on local streets
In places silently designated
We hang, deserted, in barricading fences.
We are the memorials of your courage
Fighting on local streets
Swept from bins, parks and lonely forests...
Lithakazi Mkombe, 2025

Fried Eggs

Before we were woven into being in the wombs of our mothers, a beautiful story was written. Images crafted, sounds recorded, forming a beautiful musical piece. Uniquely worded, punctuated, on cahrcoal and paper and maybe oil on canvas, creative and academic - all different, bold and subtle; loud and quiet. We were then made, woven into sculptures, living, of Eden clay. Spun by Mighty hands, moistened by Living Waters and cured by His breath. Now Living figures and parts of His speech. What could not be expressed in words was spoken in pictures, what drawings couild not capture was painted in woprds. A vision only God could see, part of His divine mystery, nothing anyone could foresee. I am 30+, no husband, no prospect and strangely no friendships too.

I remember the day I walked into a second-hand bookshop and saw a Bible for R35. If you know me you know I cannot live without one but due to unforeseen reasons my daughter and I lost all our books and Bibles. Now, as a welcome to motherhood gift my big sister Dr. Kanyisa Mcina, gifted me with a new purple and pink NIV Mother's Bible. I have treasured and read it since. I knew where to find each scripture, on what page, paragraph and what highlighter I used on it. This could be because of my photographic memory. I kept it until it was holding on by the skin of its teeth. This is when I knew I needed a new one.

Being a girl means boys will ask for your hand in marriage often. If you know me, again, you know how I get so annoyed when a man asks to take me out on a date. As I grew older I started to wonder what if I miss my God-given husband because of this? Out of my need for a new Bible; trust in a powerful God and our ability to hear Him (He is always performing miracles for me and has gifted me with various gifts of the Spirit that I never talk about because I believe they are for function not fame.) I smiled at my Lord Jesus Christ and told Him that the man He has for me will definitely know within His heart of hearts

that he must get me a Bible. This is a "Can I take you out" gesture. Then I would know and say yes. My life is very imbalanced so I do not have time for dates and social activities. I do not mind this. I got ruined as an Architecture student. I am growing and I am looking to settle down. I have had my fair share of heartache inflicted on me by various people for various reasons. Some have scorned me, leaving my heart hardened. I bring my heart to God and ask Him to work on its ill-health so I can be a better person for myself, my child and future spouse one day but remember that I am grown and people are getting more evil. As I go on about my life I am reminded of something I once wrote.

As we go on about life we get to a place where we are looking at settling down. Where we may be faced with many prospects seeking our attention for marriage, to build a life together or to build a family together but the fear of choosing wrong can be crippling. We have preferences and expectations of how things should look like and what they will be. It is good to have expectations, please have standards. Do not fall into the trap of the world telling you that your standards are too high but be mindful of being unreal in setting them.

As I studied my Theology notes by the South African Theological Seminary I came across a unit in a module entitled Husbands. Although I thought there was nothing for me in that unit, I went through it for the sake of assessments but to my surprise it enlightened me to things that I may have taken for granted. It talks about the role of the husband at home towards his wife and children, and it led me to refining my choosing compass (checklist) by adding these four points of what a godly husband should look like at the top of my checklist.

There is a lot that can be said about a husband but I will focus on these three points and elaborate on one. He should lead, protect and provide for his wife. Below are a few notes on protection that I found we take for granted in our choosing.

Can he protect me:

Physically: Protect you from harm according to his means - set measures around the house, finances and other things that you find important to bring physical security.

Psychologically: Show you respect and acceptance. Treat you in kindness and love.

Philosophically: Initiate the Lord's way into counteracting the world with all its doctrines that seek to sweep humanity to and fro.

Spiritually: Lead you pastorally at home by initiating prayer and church attendance.

These four, more than physical appearances that change as the years progress, will remain within our hearts as things we are grateful for or as desires. Then I feel safe again. Protected and ready to continue my search.

Below I write about the injustices I have faced as a woman; injustices I have seen other woman face.

My story ios different. What strikes me is that it dioes not have to be pictures or wordfs; oil or charcoal, creative or academic - we are all different. We need to treat each other with kindness and compassion. Comnplimentary to each story being told. Different in gifting and ranking, yet equally important. May our lives paint the picture painted before time. We are living figures and parts of speech;embraced in the dictionary of life - the mouth of God that spoke this world into motion.

God is vast. His attributes can never be exhausted. Since the biginning of time angels and eldres stand in awe of Him. Since the beginning of time He has forever set ablaze a wonder unimagionable tio me that forces all my being to fall flat on the ground. Made in His image. A God who since eternity has struck angels with awe ibn revelation of who He is. Through us too, He wants to reveal His glory and one person will never be enough to embody even a single attribute of His. Our stories therefore are different. Let us not gravitate towards the norm. We are unique images of Him. We are searching, building

and trying to achieve our dreams. Sometimes we run ahead of Him to stroke in lines. He is full of grace and by it He erases our errors with His love restroking His original image - a restoration of our destinies. So maybe mine is to be a spinster, or to marry and be without kids but a godly desire within me calls me unto these. Yet these are stories I cannot write on my own. In episodes of depressiobn, hurt and sometimes hope I write the poetry below to the rhythm of my frying eggs.

Charcoal Smudges

When I think about the giftings and talents God has given me and the stewardship of them I think of the story of divine humility. This involves deity who formed an earthen vessel with limitations and filled it with His life so it lives past its sell by date with the ability to steward many talents (the 10 talent servant). Earthenware susceptible to dents and cracks, yet always welcome at the table of the Potter. This Potter who, when He fixes us spuins us in control, control that can be daunting to eyes that see nearer than they should. This is who God says we are. This is who I believe I am. Handmade by God the Potter, smelling of rainy spring mornings and approved - marked by a glorious seal.

As I continue with my life I rested in knowing that the fight isn't in the size of my boots but the size of the Spirit of the Potter within me. It is He who fights. He gives me the ability to stand in mockery because He, Himself was given a crown of thorns in shame because His garments were stripped. In a lowly status because saw dust was the gist of His career.

Coffee Stains

When the sound of the flute at the constitution Hill (the place I regard as home for me because that is where all the hope of our citizens lies, the home that protects our rights and encourages us to responsibility in protecting the rights of others.) at the Human Rights Festival in March 2024 during my technical rehearsal hit the stage I held back tears. It was at that moment that I knew why I worked myself to the bone.

I continue to grow. I do not know who I will be next year but I do have bigger dreams than I had last year. I am always reminded that birds of a feather flock together. I am mindful of people I surround myself with - the things I read. You are the scents of the people that surround you. In my quest to pursue my greatest potential I have also learnt to be silent, to listen more, to let people hear my smile, feel the warmth in my absence and to show up in the mystery. UI am lovingly selective of the company I keep.

I have a new trend now - I read a lot of biographies of people who I believe have a similar background to mine but have achieved greatness beyond measure.

God has shown me kindness. I believe in teh scripture that if you submit your plans to Him, He will make your paths straight. In 2024 I could not believe that I was featured as one of 50 most influential women in South Africa. This, following my making Business and Arts South Africa's Top 20, Arts and Culture Trust Top 30, North West University Top 3 and GIBS Buisness School's Festival of Ideas Top 12. I have not even scratched the surface with what I want to achieve with my life.

I have managed to birth ON Read App - a reading and publishing app; 1 Old Note; The JuxtaPlace; Printed Honey - these are all companies that have been recognized by different companies including the most respected Durban Chamber of Commerce.

My work is mainly on justice - economic freedom for women, literacy and bridging the language gap, freedom for Africans.

I was especially honoured and i bleiev it is only the beginning when I got the opportunity to conduct research for teh United Nations Department of Economic Development when I got my interview invitation. I was drenched in the Theatre du Soleil Nomadic School for Collaborative Practices in creating Theatre and shortlisted for the North West University Pitch-Your-Business competition Pitch. Shortly after, I had an interview with the Cultural Attache (Diplomat), Secretary General and Deputy Secretary General of the French Institute of South Africa in Braamfontein for their final interview for the Cultural Projects Officer post. I saw how God's leading was amazibng.

By Imnene Mkombe
This one goes to my favourite
The one above the rest
The most awesome, kindest person
This lady she's the best
Even though this year was different
Full of troubles I might add
I'm just happy we went through it
With God's help, for this I'm glad
And even though this year was different
Not as fun as I had hoped
Thanks to you I won't detest it
I won't sit around and mope
We've lost family, we've lost friends
A lot of ties came to an end
We've still got Jesus
You've got me
So we're as happy

Preface

This is not the first book I write to you. All things I wrote to you were true, but allow me to be honest. You may wonder why I chose to write these words to you. Why I chose to lay bare to you the things that paint such an intimate story. I have always heard people ask others what their words would be if they were to write to their younger selves. I pondered this question one day and realized that I would write nothing, absolutely nothing. Having lived many years of life and managed to do the things I did I still appreciate the mystery - not knowing. (elaborate here)

Maybe not every part of it but every part that made me who I am. I have nothing to say to my younger self, nor do I have anything to say to the girl next year; but I have a lot to say about today. All I know is I have been fighting. I fight, I am very expressive and I do this using weapons closest to my heart. These are sometimes words, sometimes paint and sometimes movement.

Growing up I have always been the girl who spoke to herself or to cut holes in curtains seeking innovative ways for play. Evolving into adulthood needed me to lose this girl - which I refused to. A detriment. I believed there was no me without the things that spoke to my soul at the moment. Loudly they spoke of longevity, a guarantee to never lose relevance. They shaped my thoughts with feelings like I have been there; lived and loved. I heard them whispering songs that called me home in senses I never knew existed, covered in coffee stains, charcoal sumdges and fried eggs. I am led though. Feeling closer to the search of something deeper and something better. I understand that everyday lived could be a step closer or a step away from it, but these are my gems, they lead me, guiding me as I continue to find. A strange reality that every moment I breathe shapes are formed by the ink guiding and following our lives. Writing stories for the world to read. The writings

we did yesterday speaking of the state of th represent; nothing the past could imagine.

So I write this letter walking barefoot, immersed in art and not up to correcting my typos. Echoing in wonder of what would happen if we were not afraid or did not hide our weakness, our darkness.

There is so much more, I am a girl, black, previously disadvantaged and living in South Africa. I however walk places my feet cannot carry due to our progressive constitution. I do hope when faced with places my feet cannot carry like the gender and racial gap, my end is met by a miracle. That I understand that life, like sand on the ocean, cannot be contained or preplanned. It is unpredictable. Maybe you too have no letter for your younger self, or maybe you do. May these pages written in poetry to you help you write a story your fifty year old self will love to read - the best days of your life. Your life led by God. But I am here today.

There is a broken wooden bridge between the end of an era and the beginning of something greater - this part right here is that bridge for me. Behind you is a mountain that no one dared to climb. Glory is due even before you reach the top of it because of your work. You have done something no one was willing to. You tackled a mountain filled with heavy winds, rainfall, scorching heat and loneliness. Unpopular, isolated. Once you are at the top of it, feeling the rocks of the summit beneath your feet; you are covered in glory, glory due to you. There is a bridge you must cross - a determination of success. It is made of wood with broken pieces and torn-out strings from rope that is meant to hold it. The gender gap, the racial gap, all forms of inequality yet a progressive constitution pushes you. Bones filled with faith - for me in Jesus. You might die, you might live but across it is your reward - the reward of the climb. People never understand this moment. You have reached the mountaintop, all things should be well but they are not. They are instead worse. Never retreat. Cry, ask someone to hold your hand, close your eyes and do not forget to open them again. Continue

to walk and ignore the wind. On the other side is a plane - a pasture. It is the fruit of the breakthrough.

This is my story. I am crossing the bridge. It is that space between me receiving everything I have worked for - the funding, incubations, education, clients, etc, so I can afford my basic needs which at the moment seem like a big privilege. I have climbed the mountain. The wait between month-end to month-end when you do not know what you will eat or where you will stay but you are not retreating because you have climbed the mountain. On the other side is a pasture filled with security and rest for yourself, your children and your children's children. I am crossing the bridge with tears in my eyes; grabbing hands and closed eyes. I will remember to open them again. At the end of my closed out vision is the plane that was the price to begin with - not the glory of the mountain top but the freedom of my children. I should be free. I think I am free but I am lacking and I can attribute this to absolutely nothing. I have missed out because I am black, because I am a woman, because I am previously disadvantaged in a country with one of the most progressive constitutions in the world. Below I write my first poem for the book inspired by an art piece by Judith Mason - The Man who Sang and the Woman who Kept Silent (1998).

We are the memorials of your courage
Flying on local streets
In places silently designated
We hang, deserted, in barricading fences.
We are the memorials of your courage
Fighting on local streets
Swept from bins, parks and lonely forests...
Lithakazi Mkombe, 2025

Fried Eggs

Before we were woven into being in the wombs of our mothers, a beautiful story was written. Images crafted, sounds recorded, forming a beautiful musical piece. Uniquely worded, punctuated, on cahrcoal and paper and maybe oil on canvas, creative and academic - all different, bold and subtle; loud and quiet. We were then made, woven into sculptures, living, of Eden clay. Spun by Mighty hands, moistened by Living Waters and cured by His breath. Now Living figures and parts of His speech. What could not be expressed in words was spoken in pictures, what drawings couild not capture was painted in woprds. A vision only God could see, part of His divine mystery, nothing anyone could foresee. I am 30+, no husband, no prospect and strangely no friendships too.

I remember the day I walked into a second-hand bookshop and saw a Bible for R35. If you know me you know I cannot live without one but due to unforeseen reasons my daughter and I lost all our books and Bibles. Now, as a welcome to motherhood gift my big sister Dr. Kanyisa Mcina, gifted me with a new purple and pink NIV Mother's Bible. I have treasured and read it since. I knew where to find each scripture, on what page, paragraph and what highlighter I used on it. This could be because of my photographic memory. I kept it until it was holding on by the skin of its teeth. This is when I knew I needed a new one.

Being a girl means boys will ask for your hand in marriage often. If you know me, again, you know how I get so annoyed when a man asks to take me out on a date. As I grew older I started to wonder what if I miss my God-given husband because of this? Out of my need for a new Bible; trust in a powerful God and our ability to hear Him (He is always performing miracles for me and has gifted me with various gifts of the Spirit that I never talk about because I believe they are for function not fame.) I smiled at my Lord Jesus Christ and told Him that the man He has for me will definitely know within His heart of hearts

that he must get me a Bible. This is a "Can I take you out" gesture. Then I would know and say yes. My life is very imbalanced so I do not have time for dates and social activities. I do not mind this. I got ruined as an Architecture student. I am growing and I am looking to settle down. I have had my fair share of heartache inflicted on me by various people for various reasons. Some have scorned me, leaving my heart hardened. I bring my heart to God and ask Him to work on its ill-health so I can be a better person for myself, my child and future spouse one day but remember that I am grown and people are getting more evil. As I go on about my life I am reminded of something I once wrote.

As we go on about life we get to a place where we are looking at settling down. Where we may be faced with many prospects seeking our attention for marriage, to build a life together or to build a family together but the fear of choosing wrong can be crippling. We have preferences and expectations of how things should look like and what they will be. It is good to have expectations, please have standards. Do not fall into the trap of the world telling you that your standards are too high but be mindful of being unreal in setting them.

As I studied my Theology notes by the South African Theological Seminary I came across a unit in a module entitled Husbands. Although I thought there was nothing for me in that unit, I went through it for the sake of assessments but to my surprise it enlightened me to things that I may have taken for granted. It talks about the role of the husband at home towards his wife and children, and it led me to refining my choosing compass (checklist) by adding these four points of what a godly husband should look like at the top of my checklist.

There is a lot that can be said about a husband but I will focus on these three points and elaborate on one. He should lead, protect and provide for his wife. Below are a few notes on protection that I found we take for granted in our choosing.

Can he protect me:

Physically: Protect you from harm according to his means - set measures around the house, finances and other things that you find important to bring physical security.

Psychologically: Show you respect and acceptance. Treat you in kindness and love.

Philosophically: Initiate the Lord's way into counteracting the world with all its doctrines that seek to sweep humanity to and fro.

Spiritually: Lead you pastorally at home by initiating prayer and church attendance.

These four, more than physical appearances that change as the years progress, will remain within our hearts as things we are grateful for or as desires. Then I feel safe again. Protected and ready to continue my search.

Below I write about the injustices I have faced as a woman; injustices I have seen other woman face.

My story ios different. What strikes me is that it dioes not have to be pictures or wordfs; oil or charcoal, creative or academic - we are all different. We need to treat each other with kindness and compassion. Comnplimentary to each story being told. Different in gifting and ranking, yet equally important. May our lives paint the picture painted before time. We are living figures and parts of speech;embraced in the dictionary of life - the mouth of God that spoke this world into motion.

God is vast. His attributes can never be exhausted. Since the biginning of time angels and eldres stand in awe of Him. Since the beginning of time He has forever set ablaze a wonder unimagionable tio me that forces all my being to fall flat on the ground. Made in His image. A God who since eternity has struck angels with awe ibn revelation of who He is. Through us too, He wants to reveal His glory and one person will never be enough to embody even a single attribute of His. Our stories therefore are different. Let us not gravitate towards the norm. We are unique images of Him. We are searching, building

and trying to achieve our dreams. Sometimes we run ahead of Him to stroke in lines. He is full of grace and by it He erases our errors with His love restroking His original image - a restoration of our destinies. So maybe mine is to be a spinster, or to marry and be without kids but a godly desire within me calls me unto these. Yet these are stories I cannot write on my own. In episodes of depressiobn, hurt and sometimes hope I write the poetry below to the rhythm of my frying eggs.

Charcoal Smudges

When I think about the giftings and talents God has given me and the stewardship of them I think of the story of divine humility. This involves deity who formed an earthen vessel with limitations and filled it with His life so it lives past its sell by date with the ability to steward many talents (the 10 talent servant). Earthenware susceptible to dents and cracks, yet always welcome at the table of the Potter. This Potter who, when He fixes us spuins us in control, control that can be daunting to eyes that see nearer than they should. This is who God says we are. This is who I believe I am. Handmade by God the Potter, smelling of rainy spring mornings and approved - marked by a glorious seal.

As I continue with my life I rested in knowing that the fight isn't in the size of my boots but the size of the Spirit of the Potter within me. It is He who fights. He gives me the ability to stand in mockery because He, Himself was given a crown of thorns in shame because His garments were stripped. In a lowly status because saw dust was the gist of His career.

Coffee Stains

When the sound of the flute at the constitution Hill (the place I regard as home for me because that is where all the hope of our citizens lies, the home that protects our rights and encourages us to responsibility in protecting the rights of others.) at the Human Rights Festival in March 2024 during my technical rehearsal hit the stage I held back tears. It was at that moment that I knew why I worked myself to the bone.

I continue to grow. I do not know who I will be next year but I do have bigger dreams than I had last year. I am always reminded that birds of a feather flock together. I am mindful of people I surround myself with - the things I read. You are the scents of the people that surround you. In my quest to pursue my greatest potential I have also learnt to be silent, to listen more, to let people hear my smile, feel the warmth in my absence and to show up in the mystery. UI am lovingly selective of the company I keep.

I have a new trend now - I read a lot of biographies of people who I believe have a similar background to mine but have achieved greatness beyond measure.

God has shown me kindness. I believe in teh scripture that if you submit your plans to Him, He will make your paths straight. In 2024 I could not believe that I was featured as one of 50 most influential women in South Africa. This, following my making Business and Arts South Africa's Top 20, Arts and Culture Trust Top 30, North West University Top 3 and GIBS Buisness School's Festival of Ideas Top 12. I have not even scratched the surface with what I want to achieve with my life.

I have managed to birth ON Read App - a reading and publishing app; 1 Old Note; The JuxtaPlace; Printed Honey - these are all companies that have been recognized by different companies including the most respected Durban Chamber of Commerce.

My work is mainly on justice - economic freedom for women, literacy and bridging the language gap, freedom for Africans.

I was especially honoured and i bleiev it is only the beginning when I got the opportunity to conduct research for teh United Nations Department of Economic Development when I got my interview invitation. I was drenched in the Theatre du Soleil Nomadic School for Collaborative Practices in creating Theatre and shortlisted for the North West University Pitch-Your-Business competition Pitch. Shortly after, I had an interview with the Cultural Attache (Diplomat), Secretary General and Deputy Secretary General of the French Institute of South Africa in Braamfontein for their final interview for the Cultural Projects Officer post. I saw how God's leading was amazibng.

By Imnene Mkombe
This one goes to my favourite
The one above the rest
The most awesome, kindest person
This lady she's the best
Even though this year was different
Full of troubles I might add
I'm just happy we went through it
With God's help, for this I'm glad
And even though this year was different
Not as fun as I had hoped
Thanks to you I won't detest it
I won't sit around and mope
We've lost family, we've lost friends
A lot of ties came to an end
We've still got Jesus
You've got me
So we're as happy

Preface

This is not the first book I write to you. All things I wrote to you were true, but allow me to be honest. You may wonder why I chose to write these words to you. Why I chose to lay bare to you the things that paint such an intimate story. I have always heard people ask others what their words would be if they were to write to their younger selves. I pondered this question one day and realized that I would write nothing, absolutely nothing. Having lived many years of life and managed to do the things I did I still appreciate the mystery - not knowing. (elaborate here)

Maybe not every part of it but every part that made me who I am. I have nothing to say to my younger self, nor do I have anything to say to the girl next year; but I have a lot to say about today. All I know is I have been fighting. I fight, I am very expressive and I do this using weapons closest to my heart. These are sometimes words, sometimes paint and sometimes movement.

Growing up I have always been the girl who spoke to herself or to cut holes in curtains seeking innovative ways for play. Evolving into adulthood needed me to lose this girl - which I refused to. A detriment. I believed there was no me without the things that spoke to my soul at the moment. Loudly they spoke of longevity, a guarantee to never lose relevance. They shaped my thoughts with feelings like I have been there; lived and loved. I heard them whispering songs that called me home in senses I never knew existed, covered in coffee stains, charcoal sumdges and fried eggs. I am led though. Feeling closer to the search of something deeper and something better. I understand that everyday lived could be a step closer or a step away from it, but these are my gems, they lead me, guiding me as I continue to find. A strange reality that every moment I breathe shapes are formed by the ink guiding and following our lives. Writing stories for the world to read. The writings

we did yesterday speaking of the state of th represent; nothing the past could imagine.

So I write this letter walking barefoot, immersed in art and not up to correcting my typos. Echoing in wonder of what would happen if we were not afraid or did not hide our weakness, our darkness.

There is so much more, I am a girl, black, previously disadvantaged and living in South Africa. I however walk places my feet cannot carry due to our progressive constitution. I do hope when faced with places my feet cannot carry like the gender and racial gap, my end is met by a miracle. That I understand that life, like sand on the ocean, cannot be contained or preplanned. It is unpredictable. Maybe you too have no letter for your younger self, or maybe you do. May these pages written in poetry to you help you write a story your fifty year old self will love to read - the best days of your life. Your life led by God. But I am here today.

There is a broken wooden bridge between the end of an era and the beginning of something greater - this part right here is that bridge for me. Behind you is a mountain that no one dared to climb. Glory is due even before you reach the top of it because of your work. You have done something no one was willing to. You tackled a mountain filled with heavy winds, rainfall, scorching heat and loneliness. Unpopular, isolated. Once you are at the top of it, feeling the rocks of the summit beneath your feet; you are covered in glory, glory due to you. There is a bridge you must cross - a determination of success. It is made of wood with broken pieces and torn-out strings from rope that is meant to hold it. The gender gap, the racial gap, all forms of inequality yet a progressive constitution pushes you. Bones filled with faith - for me in Jesus. You might die, you might live but across it is your reward - the reward of the climb. People never understand this moment. You have reached the mountaintop, all things should be well but they are not. They are instead worse. Never retreat. Cry, ask someone to hold your hand, close your eyes and do not forget to open them again. Continue

to walk and ignore the wind. On the other side is a plane - a pasture. It is the fruit of the breakthrough.

This is my story. I am crossing the bridge. It is that space between me receiving everything I have worked for - the funding, incubations, education, clients, etc, so I can afford my basic needs which at the moment seem like a big privilege. I have climbed the mountain. The wait between month-end to month-end when you do not know what you will eat or where you will stay but you are not retreating because you have climbed the mountain. On the other side is a pasture filled with security and rest for yourself, your children and your children's children. I am crossing the bridge with tears in my eyes; grabbing hands and closed eyes. I will remember to open them again. At the end of my closed out vision is the plane that was the price to begin with - not the glory of the mountain top but the freedom of my children. I should be free. I think I am free but I am lacking and I can attribute this to absolutely nothing. I have missed out because I am black, because I am a woman, because I am previously disadvantaged in a country with one of the most progressive constitutions in the world. Below I write my first poem for the book inspired by an art piece by Judith Mason - The Man who Sang and the Woman who Kept Silent (1998).

We are the memorials of your courage
Flying on local streets
In places silently designated
We hang, deserted, in barricading fences.
We are the memorials of your courage
Fighting on local streets
Swept from bins, parks and lonely forests...
Lithakazi Mkombe, 2025

Fried Eggs

Before we were woven into being in the wombs of our mothers, a beautiful story was written. Images crafted, sounds recorded, forming a beautiful musical piece. Uniquely worded, punctuated, on cahrcoal and paper and maybe oil on canvas, creative and academic - all different, bold and subtle; loud and quiet. We were then made, woven into sculptures, living, of Eden clay. Spun by Mighty hands, moistened by Living Waters and cured by His breath. Now Living figures and parts of His speech. What could not be expressed in words was spoken in pictures, what drawings couild not capture was painted in woprds. A vision only God could see, part of His divine mystery, nothing anyone could foresee. I am 30+, no husband, no prospect and strangely no friendships too.

I remember the day I walked into a second-hand bookshop and saw a Bible for R35. If you know me you know I cannot live without one but due to unforeseen reasons my daughter and I lost all our books and Bibles. Now, as a welcome to motherhood gift my big sister Dr. Kanyisa Mcina, gifted me with a new purple and pink NIV Mother's Bible. I have treasured and read it since. I knew where to find each scripture, on what page, paragraph and what highlighter I used on it. This could be because of my photographic memory. I kept it until it was holding on by the skin of its teeth. This is when I knew I needed a new one.

Being a girl means boys will ask for your hand in marriage often. If you know me, again, you know how I get so annoyed when a man asks to take me out on a date. As I grew older I started to wonder what if I miss my God-given husband because of this? Out of my need for a new Bible; trust in a powerful God and our ability to hear Him (He is always performing miracles for me and has gifted me with various gifts of the Spirit that I never talk about because I believe they are for function not fame.) I smiled at my Lord Jesus Christ and told Him that the man He has for me will definitely know within His heart of hearts

that he must get me a Bible. This is a "Can I take you out" gesture. Then I would know and say yes. My life is very imbalanced so I do not have time for dates and social activities. I do not mind this. I got ruined as an Architecture student. I am growing and I am looking to settle down. I have had my fair share of heartache inflicted on me by various people for various reasons. Some have scorned me, leaving my heart hardened. I bring my heart to God and ask Him to work on its ill-health so I can be a better person for myself, my child and future spouse one day but remember that I am grown and people are getting more evil. As I go on about my life I am reminded of something I once wrote.

As we go on about life we get to a place where we are looking at settling down. Where we may be faced with many prospects seeking our attention for marriage, to build a life together or to build a family together but the fear of choosing wrong can be crippling. We have preferences and expectations of how things should look like and what they will be. It is good to have expectations, please have standards. Do not fall into the trap of the world telling you that your standards are too high but be mindful of being unreal in setting them.

As I studied my Theology notes by the South African Theological Seminary I came across a unit in a module entitled Husbands. Although I thought there was nothing for me in that unit, I went through it for the sake of assessments but to my surprise it enlightened me to things that I may have taken for granted. It talks about the role of the husband at home towards his wife and children, and it led me to refining my choosing compass (checklist) by adding these four points of what a godly husband should look like at the top of my checklist.

There is a lot that can be said about a husband but I will focus on these three points and elaborate on one. He should lead, protect and provide for his wife. Below are a few notes on protection that I found we take for granted in our choosing.

Can he protect me:

Physically: Protect you from harm according to his means - set measures around the house, finances and other things that you find important to bring physical security.

Psychologically: Show you respect and acceptance. Treat you in kindness and love.

Philosophically: Initiate the Lord's way into counteracting the world with all its doctrines that seek to sweep humanity to and fro.

Spiritually: Lead you pastorally at home by initiating prayer and church attendance.

These four, more than physical appearances that change as the years progress, will remain within our hearts as things we are grateful for or as desires. Then I feel safe again. Protected and ready to continue my search.

Below I write about the injustices I have faced as a woman; injustices I have seen other woman face.

My story ios different. What strikes me is that it dioes not have to be pictures or wordfs; oil or charcoal, creative or academic - we are all different. We need to treat each other with kindness and compassion. Comnplimentary to each story being told. Different in gifting and ranking, yet equally important. May our lives paint the picture painted before time. We are living figures and parts of speech;embraced in the dictionary of life - the mouth of God that spoke this world into motion.

God is vast. His attributes can never be exhausted. Since the biginning of time angels and eldres stand in awe of Him. Since the beginning of time He has forever set ablaze a wonder unimagionable tio me that forces all my being to fall flat on the ground. Made in His image. A God who since eternity has struck angels with awe ibn revelation of who He is. Through us too, He wants to reveal His glory and one person will never be enough to embody even a single attribute of His. Our stories therefore are different. Let us not gravitate towards the norm. We are unique images of Him. We are searching, building

and trying to achieve our dreams. Sometimes we run ahead of Him to stroke in lines. He is full of grace and by it He erases our errors with His love restroking His original image - a restoration of our destinies. So maybe mine is to be a spinster, or to marry and be without kids but a godly desire within me calls me unto these. Yet these are stories I cannot write on my own. In episodes of depressiobn, hurt and sometimes hope I write the poetry below to the rhythm of my frying eggs.

Charcoal Smudges

When I think about the giftings and talents God has given me and the stewardship of them I think of the story of divine humility. This involves deity who formed an earthen vessel with limitations and filled it with His life so it lives past its sell by date with the ability to steward many talents (the 10 talent servant). Earthenware susceptible to dents and cracks, yet always welcome at the table of the Potter. This Potter who, when He fixes us spuins us in control, control that can be daunting to eyes that see nearer than they should. This is who God says we are. This is who I believe I am. Handmade by God the Potter, smelling of rainy spring mornings and approved - marked by a glorious seal.

As I continue with my life I rested in knowing that the fight isn't in the size of my boots but the size of the Spirit of the Potter within me. It is He who fights. He gives me the ability to stand in mockery because He, Himself was given a crown of thorns in shame because His garments were stripped. In a lowly status because saw dust was the gist of His career.

Coffee Stains

When the sound of the flute at the constitution Hill (the place I regard as home for me because that is where all the hope of our citizens lies, the home that protects our rights and encourages us to responsibility in protecting the rights of others.) at the Human Rights Festival in March 2024 during my technical rehearsal hit the stage I held back tears. It was at that moment that I knew why I worked myself to the bone.

I continue to grow. I do not know who I will be next year but I do have bigger dreams than I had last year. I am always reminded that birds of a feather flock together. I am mindful of people I surround myself with - the things I read. You are the scents of the people that surround you. In my quest to pursue my greatest potential I have also learnt to be silent, to listen more, to let people hear my smile, feel the warmth in my absence and to show up in the mystery. UI am lovingly selective of the company I keep.

I have a new trend now - I read a lot of biographies of people who I believe have a similar background to mine but have achieved greatness beyond measure.

God has shown me kindness. I believe in teh scripture that if you submit your plans to Him, He will make your paths straight. In 2024 I could not believe that I was featured as one of 50 most influential women in South Africa. This, following my making Business and Arts South Africa's Top 20, Arts and Culture Trust Top 30, North West University Top 3 and GIBS Buisness School's Festival of Ideas Top 12. I have not even scratched the surface with what I want to achieve with my life.

I have managed to birth ON Read App - a reading and publishing app; 1 Old Note; The JuxtaPlace; Printed Honey - these are all companies that have been recognized by different companies including the most respected Durban Chamber of Commerce.

My work is mainly on justice - economic freedom for women, literacy and bridging the language gap, freedom for Africans.

I was especially honoured and i bleiev it is only the beginning when I got the opportunity to conduct research for teh United Nations Department of Economic Development when I got my interview invitation. I was drenched in the Theatre du Soleil Nomadic School for Collaborative Practices in creating Theatre and shortlisted for the North West University Pitch-Your-Business competition Pitch. Shortly after, I had an interview with the Cultural Attache (Diplomat), Secretary General and Deputy Secretary General of the French Institute of South Africa in Braamfontein for their final interview for the Cultural Projects Officer post. I saw how God's leading was amazibng.

By Imnene Mkombe
This one goes to my favourite
The one above the rest
The most awesome, kindest person
This lady she's the best
Even though this year was different
Full of troubles I might add
I'm just happy we went through it
With God's help, for this I'm glad
And even though this year was different
Not as fun as I had hoped
Thanks to you I won't detest it
I won't sit around and mope
We've lost family, we've lost friends
A lot of ties came to an end
We've still got Jesus
You've got me
So we're as happy

Preface

This is not the first book I write to you. All things I wrote to you were true, but allow me to be honest. You may wonder why I chose to write these words to you. Why I chose to lay bare to you the things that paint such an intimate story. I have always heard people ask others what their words would be if they were to write to their younger selves. I pondered this question one day and realized that I would write nothing, absolutely nothing. Having lived many years of life and managed to do the things I did I still appreciate the mystery - not knowing. (elaborate here)

Maybe not every part of it but every part that made me who I am. I have nothing to say to my younger self, nor do I have anything to say to the girl next year; but I have a lot to say about today. All I know is I have been fighting. I fight, I am very expressive and I do this using weapons closest to my heart. These are sometimes words, sometimes paint and sometimes movement.

Growing up I have always been the girl who spoke to herself or to cut holes in curtains seeking innovative ways for play. Evolving into adulthood needed me to lose this girl - which I refused to. A detriment. I believed there was no me without the things that spoke to my soul at the moment. Loudly they spoke of longevity, a guarantee to never lose relevance. They shaped my thoughts with feelings like I have been there; lived and loved. I heard them whispering songs that called me home in senses I never knew existed, covered in coffee stains, charcoal sumdges and fried eggs. I am led though. Feeling closer to the search of something deeper and something better. I understand that everyday lived could be a step closer or a step away from it, but these are my gems, they lead me, guiding me as I continue to find. A strange reality that every moment I breathe shapes are formed by the ink guiding and following our lives. Writing stories for the world to read. The writings

we did yesterday speaking of the state of th represent; nothing the past could imagine.

So I write this letter walking barefoot, immersed in art and not up to correcting my typos. Echoing in wonder of what would happen if we were not afraid or did not hide our weakness, our darkness.

There is so much more, I am a girl, black, previously disadvantaged and living in South Africa. I however walk places my feet cannot carry due to our progressive constitution. I do hope when faced with places my feet cannot carry like the gender and racial gap, my end is met by a miracle. That I understand that life, like sand on the ocean, cannot be contained or preplanned. It is unpredictable. Maybe you too have no letter for your younger self, or maybe you do. May these pages written in poetry to you help you write a story your fifty year old self will love to read - the best days of your life. Your life led by God. But I am here today.

There is a broken wooden bridge between the end of an era and the beginning of something greater - this part right here is that bridge for me. Behind you is a mountain that no one dared to climb. Glory is due even before you reach the top of it because of your work. You have done something no one was willing to. You tackled a mountain filled with heavy winds, rainfall, scorching heat and loneliness. Unpopular, isolated. Once you are at the top of it, feeling the rocks of the summit beneath your feet; you are covered in glory, glory due to you. There is a bridge you must cross - a determination of success. It is made of wood with broken pieces and torn-out strings from rope that is meant to hold it. The gender gap, the racial gap, all forms of inequality yet a progressive constitution pushes you. Bones filled with faith - for me in Jesus. You might die, you might live but across it is your reward - the reward of the climb. People never understand this moment. You have reached the mountaintop, all things should be well but they are not. They are instead worse. Never retreat. Cry, ask someone to hold your hand, close your eyes and do not forget to open them again. Continue

to walk and ignore the wind. On the other side is a plane - a pasture. It is the fruit of the breakthrough.

This is my story. I am crossing the bridge. It is that space between me receiving everything I have worked for - the funding, incubations, education, clients, etc, so I can afford my basic needs which at the moment seem like a big privilege. I have climbed the mountain. The wait between month-end to month-end when you do not know what you will eat or where you will stay but you are not retreating because you have climbed the mountain. On the other side is a pasture filled with security and rest for yourself, your children and your children's children. I am crossing the bridge with tears in my eyes; grabbing hands and closed eyes. I will remember to open them again. At the end of my closed out vision is the plane that was the price to begin with - not the glory of the mountain top but the freedom of my children. I should be free. I think I am free but I am lacking and I can attribute this to absolutely nothing. I have missed out because I am black, because I am a woman, because I am previously disadvantaged in a country with one of the most progressive constitutions in the world. Below I write my first poem for the book inspired by an art piece by Judith Mason - The Man who Sang and the Woman who Kept Silent (1998).

We are the memorials of your courage
Flying on local streets
In places silently designated
We hang, deserted, in barricading fences.
We are the memorials of your courage
Fighting on local streets
Swept from bins, parks and lonely forests...
Lithakazi Mkombe, 2025

Fried Eggs

Before we were woven into being in the wombs of our mothers, a beautiful story was written. Images crafted, sounds recorded, forming a beautiful musical piece. Uniquely worded, punctuated, on cahrcoal and paper and maybe oil on canvas, creative and academic - all different, bold and subtle; loud and quiet. We were then made, woven into sculptures, living, of Eden clay. Spun by Mighty hands, moistened by Living Waters and cured by His breath. Now Living figures and parts of His speech. What could not be expressed in words was spoken in pictures, what drawings couild not capture was painted in woprds. A vision only God could see, part of His divine mystery, nothing anyone could foresee. I am 30+, no husband, no prospect and strangely no friendships too.

I remember the day I walked into a second-hand bookshop and saw a Bible for R35. If you know me you know I cannot live without one but due to unforeseen reasons my daughter and I lost all our books and Bibles. Now, as a welcome to motherhood gift my big sister Dr. Kanyisa Mcina, gifted me with a new purple and pink NIV Mother's Bible. I have treasured and read it since. I knew where to find each scripture, on what page, paragraph and what highlighter I used on it. This could be because of my photographic memory. I kept it until it was holding on by the skin of its teeth. This is when I knew I needed a new one.

Being a girl means boys will ask for your hand in marriage often. If you know me, again, you know how I get so annoyed when a man asks to take me out on a date. As I grew older I started to wonder what if I miss my God-given husband because of this? Out of my need for a new Bible; trust in a powerful God and our ability to hear Him (He is always performing miracles for me and has gifted me with various gifts of the Spirit that I never talk about because I believe they are for function not fame.) I smiled at my Lord Jesus Christ and told Him that the man He has for me will definitely know within His heart of hearts

that he must get me a Bible. This is a "Can I take you out" gesture. Then I would know and say yes. My life is very imbalanced so I do not have time for dates and social activities. I do not mind this. I got ruined as an Architecture student. I am growing and I am looking to settle down. I have had my fair share of heartache inflicted on me by various people for various reasons. Some have scorned me, leaving my heart hardened. I bring my heart to God and ask Him to work on its ill-health so I can be a better person for myself, my child and future spouse one day but remember that I am grown and people are getting more evil. As I go on about my life I am reminded of something I once wrote.

As we go on about life we get to a place where we are looking at settling down. Where we may be faced with many prospects seeking our attention for marriage, to build a life together or to build a family together but the fear of choosing wrong can be crippling. We have preferences and expectations of how things should look like and what they will be. It is good to have expectations, please have standards. Do not fall into the trap of the world telling you that your standards are too high but be mindful of being unreal in setting them.

As I studied my Theology notes by the South African Theological Seminary I came across a unit in a module entitled Husbands. Although I thought there was nothing for me in that unit, I went through it for the sake of assessments but to my surprise it enlightened me to things that I may have taken for granted. It talks about the role of the husband at home towards his wife and children, and it led me to refining my choosing compass (checklist) by adding these four points of what a godly husband should look like at the top of my checklist.

There is a lot that can be said about a husband but I will focus on these three points and elaborate on one. He should lead, protect and provide for his wife. Below are a few notes on protection that I found we take for granted in our choosing.

Can he protect me:

Physically: Protect you from harm according to his means - set measures around the house, finances and other things that you find important to bring physical security.

Psychologically: Show you respect and acceptance. Treat you in kindness and love.

Philosophically: Initiate the Lord's way into counteracting the world with all its doctrines that seek to sweep humanity to and fro.

Spiritually: Lead you pastorally at home by initiating prayer and church attendance.

These four, more than physical appearances that change as the years progress, will remain within our hearts as things we are grateful for or as desires. Then I feel safe again. Protected and ready to continue my search.

Below I write about the injustices I have faced as a woman; injustices I have seen other woman face.

My story ios different. What strikes me is that it dioes not have to be pictures or wordfs; oil or charcoal, creative or academic - we are all different. We need to treat each other with kindness and compassion. Comnplimentary to each story being told. Different in gifting and ranking, yet equally important. May our lives paint the picture painted before time. We are living figures and parts of speech;embraced in the dictionary of life - the mouth of God that spoke this world into motion.

God is vast. His attributes can never be exhausted. Since the biginning of time angels and eldres stand in awe of Him. Since the beginning of time He has forever set ablaze a wonder unimagionable tio me that forces all my being to fall flat on the ground. Made in His image. A God who since eternity has struck angels with awe ibn revelation of who He is. Through us too, He wants to reveal His glory and one person will never be enough to embody even a single attribute of His. Our stories therefore are different. Let us not gravitate towards the norm. We are unique images of Him. We are searching, building

and trying to achieve our dreams. Sometimes we run ahead of Him to stroke in lines. He is full of grace and by it He erases our errors with His love restroking His original image - a restoration of our destinies. So maybe mine is to be a spinster, or to marry and be without kids but a godly desire within me calls me unto these. Yet these are stories I cannot write on my own. In episodes of depressiobn, hurt and sometimes hope I write the poetry below to the rhythm of my frying eggs.

Charcoal Smudges

When I think about the giftings and talents God has given me and the stewardship of them I think of the story of divine humility. This involves deity who formed an earthen vessel with limitations and filled it with His life so it lives past its sell by date with the ability to steward many talents (the 10 talent servant). Earthenware susceptible to dents and cracks, yet always welcome at the table of the Potter. This Potter who, when He fixes us spuins us in control, control that can be daunting to eyes that see nearer than they should. This is who God says we are. This is who I believe I am. Handmade by God the Potter, smelling of rainy spring mornings and approved - marked by a glorious seal.

As I continue with my life I rested in knowing that the fight isn't in the size of my boots but the size of the Spirit of the Potter within me. It is He who fights. He gives me the ability to stand in mockery because He, Himself was given a crown of thorns in shame because His garments were stripped. In a lowly status because saw dust was the gist of His career.

Coffee Stains

When the sound of the flute at the constitution Hill (the place I regard as home for me because that is where all the hope of our citizens lies, the home that protects our rights and encourages us to responsibility in protecting the rights of others.) at the Human Rights Festival in March 2024 during my technical rehearsal hit the stage I held back tears. It was at that moment that I knew why I worked myself to the bone.

I continue to grow. I do not know who I will be next year but I do have bigger dreams than I had last year. I am always reminded that birds of a feather flock together. I am mindful of people I surround myself with - the things I read. You are the scents of the people that surround you. In my quest to pursue my greatest potential I have also learnt to be silent, to listen more, to let people hear my smile, feel the warmth in my absence and to show up in the mystery. UI am lovingly selective of the company I keep.

I have a new trend now - I read a lot of biographies of people who I believe have a similar background to mine but have achieved greatness beyond measure.

God has shown me kindness. I believe in teh scripture that if you submit your plans to Him, He will make your paths straight. In 2024 I could not believe that I was featured as one of 50 most influential women in South Africa. This, following my making Business and Arts South Africa's Top 20, Arts and Culture Trust Top 30, North West University Top 3 and GIBS Buisness School's Festival of Ideas Top 12. I have not even scratched the surface with what I want to achieve with my life.

I have managed to birth ON Read App - a reading and publishing app; 1 Old Note; The JuxtaPlace; Printed Honey - these are all companies that have been recognized by different companies including the most respected Durban Chamber of Commerce.

My work is mainly on justice - economic freedom for women, literacy and bridging the language gap, freedom for Africans.

I was especially honoured and i bleiev it is only the beginning when I got the opportunity to conduct research for teh United Nations Department of Economic Development when I got my interview invitation. I was drenched in the Theatre du Soleil Nomadic School for Collaborative Practices in creating Theatre and shortlisted for the North West University Pitch-Your-Business competition Pitch. Shortly after, I had an interview with the Cultural Attache (Diplomat), Secretary General and Deputy Secretary General of the French Institute of South Africa in Braamfontein for their final interview for the Cultural Projects Officer post. I saw how God's leading was amazibng.

By Imnene Mkombe
This one goes to my favourite
The one above the rest
The most awesome, kindest person
This lady she's the best
Even though this year was different
Full of troubles I might add
I'm just happy we went through it
With God's help, for this I'm glad
And even though this year was different
Not as fun as I had hoped
Thanks to you I won't detest it
I won't sit around and mope
We've lost family, we've lost friends
A lot of ties came to an end
We've still got Jesus
You've got me
So we're as happy

Preface

This is not the first book I write to you. All things I wrote to you were true, but allow me to be honest. You may wonder why I chose to write these words to you. Why I chose to lay bare to you the things that paint such an intimate story. I have always heard people ask others what their words would be if they were to write to their younger selves. I pondered this question one day and realized that I would write nothing, absolutely nothing. Having lived many years of life and managed to do the things I did I still appreciate the mystery - not knowing. (elaborate here)

Maybe not every part of it but every part that made me who I am. I have nothing to say to my younger self, nor do I have anything to say to the girl next year; but I have a lot to say about today. All I know is I have been fighting. I fight, I am very expressive and I do this using weapons closest to my heart. These are sometimes words, sometimes paint and sometimes movement.

Growing up I have always been the girl who spoke to herself or to cut holes in curtains seeking innovative ways for play. Evolving into adulthood needed me to lose this girl - which I refused to. A detriment. I believed there was no me without the things that spoke to my soul at the moment. Loudly they spoke of longevity, a guarantee to never lose relevance. They shaped my thoughts with feelings like I have been there; lived and loved. I heard them whispering songs that called me home in senses I never knew existed, covered in coffee stains, charcoal sumdges and fried eggs. I am led though. Feeling closer to the search of something deeper and something better. I understand that everyday lived could be a step closer or a step away from it, but these are my gems, they lead me, guiding me as I continue to find. A strange reality that every moment I breathe shapes are formed by the ink guiding and following our lives. Writing stories for the world to read. The writings

we did yesterday speaking of the state of th represent; nothing the past could imagine.

So I write this letter walking barefoot, immersed in art and not up to correcting my typos. Echoing in wonder of what would happen if we were not afraid or did not hide our weakness, our darkness.

There is so much more, I am a girl, black, previously disadvantaged and living in South Africa. I however walk places my feet cannot carry due to our progressive constitution. I do hope when faced with places my feet cannot carry like the gender and racial gap, my end is met by a miracle. That I understand that life, like sand on the ocean, cannot be contained or preplanned. It is unpredictable. Maybe you too have no letter for your younger self, or maybe you do. May these pages written in poetry to you help you write a story your fifty year old self will love to read - the best days of your life. Your life led by God. But I am here today.

There is a broken wooden bridge between the end of an era and the beginning of something greater - this part right here is that bridge for me. Behind you is a mountain that no one dared to climb. Glory is due even before you reach the top of it because of your work. You have done something no one was willing to. You tackled a mountain filled with heavy winds, rainfall, scorching heat and loneliness. Unpopular, isolated. Once you are at the top of it, feeling the rocks of the summit beneath your feet; you are covered in glory, glory due to you. There is a bridge you must cross - a determination of success. It is made of wood with broken pieces and torn-out strings from rope that is meant to hold it. The gender gap, the racial gap, all forms of inequality yet a progressive constitution pushes you. Bones filled with faith - for me in Jesus. You might die, you might live but across it is your reward - the reward of the climb. People never understand this moment. You have reached the mountaintop, all things should be well but they are not. They are instead worse. Never retreat. Cry, ask someone to hold your hand, close your eyes and do not forget to open them again. Continue

to walk and ignore the wind. On the other side is a plane - a pasture. It is the fruit of the breakthrough.

This is my story. I am crossing the bridge. It is that space between me receiving everything I have worked for - the funding, incubations, education, clients, etc, so I can afford my basic needs which at the moment seem like a big privilege. I have climbed the mountain. The wait between month-end to month-end when you do not know what you will eat or where you will stay but you are not retreating because you have climbed the mountain. On the other side is a pasture filled with security and rest for yourself, your children and your children's children. I am crossing the bridge with tears in my eyes; grabbing hands and closed eyes. I will remember to open them again. At the end of my closed out vision is the plane that was the price to begin with - not the glory of the mountain top but the freedom of my children. I should be free. I think I am free but I am lacking and I can attribute this to absolutely nothing. I have missed out because I am black, because I am a woman, because I am previously disadvantaged in a country with one of the most progressive constitutions in the world. Below I write my first poem for the book inspired by an art piece by Judith Mason - The Man who Sang and the Woman who Kept Silent (1998).

We are the memorials of your courage
Flying on local streets
In places silently designated
We hang, deserted, in barricading fences.
We are the memorials of your courage
Fighting on local streets
Swept from bins, parks and lonely forests...
Lithakazi Mkombe, 2025

Fried Eggs

Before we were woven into being in the wombs of our mothers, a beautiful story was written. Images crafted, sounds recorded, forming a beautiful musical piece. Uniquely worded, punctuated, on cahrcoal and paper and maybe oil on canvas, creative and academic - all different, bold and subtle; loud and quiet. We were then made, woven into sculptures, living, of Eden clay. Spun by Mighty hands, moistened by Living Waters and cured by His breath. Now Living figures and parts of His speech. What could not be expressed in words was spoken in pictures, what drawings couild not capture was painted in woprds. A vision only God could see, part of His divine mystery, nothing anyone could foresee. I am 30+, no husband, no prospect and strangely no friendships too.

I remember the day I walked into a second-hand bookshop and saw a Bible for R35. If you know me you know I cannot live without one but due to unforeseen reasons my daughter and I lost all our books and Bibles. Now, as a welcome to motherhood gift my big sister Dr. Kanyisa Mcina, gifted me with a new purple and pink NIV Mother's Bible. I have treasured and read it since. I knew where to find each scripture, on what page, paragraph and what highlighter I used on it. This could be because of my photographic memory. I kept it until it was holding on by the skin of its teeth. This is when I knew I needed a new one.

Being a girl means boys will ask for your hand in marriage often. If you know me, again, you know how I get so annoyed when a man asks to take me out on a date. As I grew older I started to wonder what if I miss my God-given husband because of this? Out of my need for a new Bible; trust in a powerful God and our ability to hear Him (He is always performing miracles for me and has gifted me with various gifts of the Spirit that I never talk about because I believe they are for function not fame.) I smiled at my Lord Jesus Christ and told Him that the man He has for me will definitely know within His heart of hearts

that he must get me a Bible. This is a "Can I take you out" gesture. Then I would know and say yes. My life is very imbalanced so I do not have time for dates and social activities. I do not mind this. I got ruined as an Architecture student. I am growing and I am looking to settle down. I have had my fair share of heartache inflicted on me by various people for various reasons. Some have scorned me, leaving my heart hardened. I bring my heart to God and ask Him to work on its ill-health so I can be a better person for myself, my child and future spouse one day but remember that I am grown and people are getting more evil. As I go on about my life I am reminded of something I once wrote.

As we go on about life we get to a place where we are looking at settling down. Where we may be faced with many prospects seeking our attention for marriage, to build a life together or to build a family together but the fear of choosing wrong can be crippling. We have preferences and expectations of how things should look like and what they will be. It is good to have expectations, please have standards. Do not fall into the trap of the world telling you that your standards are too high but be mindful of being unreal in setting them.

As I studied my Theology notes by the South African Theological Seminary I came across a unit in a module entitled Husbands. Although I thought there was nothing for me in that unit, I went through it for the sake of assessments but to my surprise it enlightened me to things that I may have taken for granted. It talks about the role of the husband at home towards his wife and children, and it led me to refining my choosing compass (checklist) by adding these four points of what a godly husband should look like at the top of my checklist.

There is a lot that can be said about a husband but I will focus on these three points and elaborate on one. He should lead, protect and provide for his wife. Below are a few notes on protection that I found we take for granted in our choosing.

Can he protect me:

Physically: Protect you from harm according to his means - set measures around the house, finances and other things that you find important to bring physical security.

Psychologically: Show you respect and acceptance. Treat you in kindness and love.

Philosophically: Initiate the Lord's way into counteracting the world with all its doctrines that seek to sweep humanity to and fro.

Spiritually: Lead you pastorally at home by initiating prayer and church attendance.

These four, more than physical appearances that change as the years progress, will remain within our hearts as things we are grateful for or as desires. Then I feel safe again. Protected and ready to continue my search.

Below I write about the injustices I have faced as a woman; injustices I have seen other woman face.

My story ios different. What strikes me is that it dioes not have to be pictures or wordfs; oil or charcoal, creative or academic - we are all different. We need to treat each other with kindness and compassion. Comnplimentary to each story being told. Different in gifting and ranking, yet equally important. May our lives paint the picture painted before time. We are living figures and parts of speech;embraced in the dictionary of life - the mouth of God that spoke this world into motion.

God is vast. His attributes can never be exhausted. Since the biginning of time angels and eldres stand in awe of Him. Since the beginning of time He has forever set ablaze a wonder unimagionable tio me that forces all my being to fall flat on the ground. Made in His image. A God who since eternity has struck angels with awe ibn revelation of who He is. Through us too, He wants to reveal His glory and one person will never be enough to embody even a single attribute of His. Our stories therefore are different. Let us not gravitate towards the norm. We are unique images of Him. We are searching, building

and trying to achieve our dreams. Sometimes we run ahead of Him to stroke in lines. He is full of grace and by it He erases our errors with His love restroking His original image - a restoration of our destinies. So maybe mine is to be a spinster, or to marry and be without kids but a godly desire within me calls me unto these. Yet these are stories I cannot write on my own. In episodes of depressiobn, hurt and sometimes hope I write the poetry below to the rhythm of my frying eggs.

Charcoal Smudges

When I think about the giftings and talents God has given me and the stewardship of them I think of the story of divine humility. This involves deity who formed an earthen vessel with limitations and filled it with His life so it lives past its sell by date with the ability to steward many talents (the 10 talent servant). Earthenware susceptible to dents and cracks, yet always welcome at the table of the Potter. This Potter who, when He fixes us spuins us in control, control that can be daunting to eyes that see nearer than they should. This is who God says we are. This is who I believe I am. Handmade by God the Potter, smelling of rainy spring mornings and approved - marked by a glorious seal.

As I continue with my life I rested in knowing that the fight isn't in the size of my boots but the size of the Spirit of the Potter within me. It is He who fights. He gives me the ability to stand in mockery because He, Himself was given a crown of thorns in shame because His garments were stripped. In a lowly status because saw dust was the gist of His career.

Coffee Stains

When the sound of the flute at the constitution Hill (the place I regard as home for me because that is where all the hope of our citizens lies, the home that protects our rights and encourages us to responsibility in protecting the rights of others.) at the Human Rights Festival in March 2024 during my technical rehearsal hit the stage I held back tears. It was at that moment that I knew why I worked myself to the bone.

I continue to grow. I do not know who I will be next year but I do have bigger dreams than I had last year. I am always reminded that birds of a feather flock together. I am mindful of people I surround myself with - the things I read. You are the scents of the people that surround you. In my quest to pursue my greatest potential I have also learnt to be silent, to listen more, to let people hear my smile, feel the warmth in my absence and to show up in the mystery. UI am lovingly selective of the company I keep.

I have a new trend now - I read a lot of biographies of people who I believe have a similar background to mine but have achieved greatness beyond measure.

God has shown me kindness. I believe in teh scripture that if you submit your plans to Him, He will make your paths straight. In 2024 I could not believe that I was featured as one of 50 most influential women in South Africa. This, following my making Business and Arts South Africa's Top 20, Arts and Culture Trust Top 30, North West University Top 3 and GIBS Buisness School's Festival of Ideas Top 12. I have not even scratched the surface with what I want to achieve with my life.

I have managed to birth ON Read App - a reading and publishing app; 1 Old Note; The JuxtaPlace; Printed Honey - these are all companies that have been recognized by different companies including the most respected Durban Chamber of Commerce.

My work is mainly on justice - economic freedom for women, literacy and bridging the language gap, freedom for Africans.

I was especially honoured and i bleiev it is only the beginning when I got the opportunity to conduct research for teh United Nations Department of Economic Development when I got my interview invitation. I was drenched in the Theatre du Soleil Nomadic School for Collaborative Practices in creating Theatre and shortlisted for the North West University Pitch-Your-Business competition Pitch. Shortly after, I had an interview with the Cultural Attache (Diplomat), Secretary General and Deputy Secretary General of the French Institute of South Africa in Braamfontein for their final interview for the Cultural Projects Officer post. I saw how God's leading was amazibng.

By Imnene Mkombe
This one goes to my favourite
The one above the rest
The most awesome, kindest person
This lady she's the best
Even though this year was different
Full of troubles I might add
I'm just happy we went through it
With God's help, for this I'm glad
And even though this year was different
Not as fun as I had hoped
Thanks to you I won't detest it
I won't sit around and mope
We've lost family, we've lost friends
A lot of ties came to an end
We've still got Jesus
You've got me
So we're as happy

Also by Lithakazi Mkombe

Coffee Stains, Charcoal Smudges and Fried Eggs

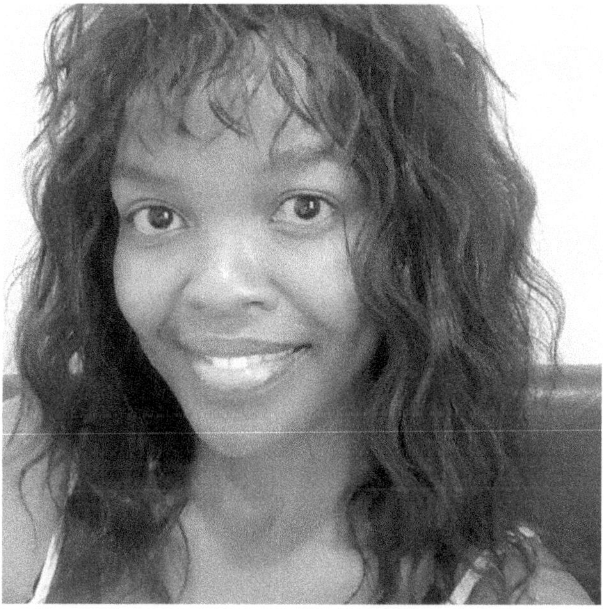

About the Author

Lithakazi Mkombe is an artist, entrepreneur and strategist who has received various recognition for her work. She studied Architectural Technology at the Durban University of Technology. Her passion for art opened various doors for her including the Nomadic School she attended with the French Theatre ensemble - Theatre du Soleil, and Poetic Inquiry training through the Human Sciences Research Council. She has written plays that have shown at various theatres.

www.ingramcontent.com/pod-product-compliance
Ingram Content Group UK Ltd.
Pitfield, Milton Keynes, MK11 3LW, UK
UKHW041949110325
456116UK00001B/15

* 9 7 8 1 0 3 7 0 3 3 0 5 6 *